REX MASTURBATORQUE

King
Nicholas
and the
Copeman
Empire

To Zara

King Nicholas and the Copeman Empire

Nick Copeman

EBURY
PRESS

1 3 5 7 9 10 8 6 4 2

Copyright © 2005 Nick Copeman

Nick Copeman has asserted his moral right to be identified
as the author of this work in accordance with the Copyright,
Designs and Patents Act 1988.

All rights reserved. No part of this publication may be reproduced,
stored in a retrieval system, or transmitted in any form or by any
means, electronic, mechanical, photocopying or otherwise
without the prior permission of the copyright owner.

First published 2005 by Ebury Press,
An imprint of Random House,
20 Vauxhall Bridge Road, London SW1V 2SA

Random House Australia (Pty) Limited
20 Alfred Street, Milsons Point, Sydney,
New South Wales 2061, Australia

Random House New Zealand Limited
18 Poland Road, Glenfield, Auckland 10, New Zealand

Random House South Africa (Pty) Limited
Endulini, 5a Jubilee Road, Parktown 2193, South Africa

The Random House Group Limited Reg. No. 954009

www.randomhouse.co.uk

Printed and bound in Great Britain by Mackays of Chatham plc, Kent

A CIP catalogue record for this book is
available from the British Library.

Cover designed by Jon Gray
Interior by seagulls

ISBN 0 0918 9920 6

Contents

Honours List

His Majesty would like to thank and honour:
Sir Andrew Goodfellow KZ (Ebury Press),
for Services to Literature
Roy Boy OCE, for Services to Lay-By Catering
Chris Marshall OCE, for Services to Barbering
Michael Gilmore MCE, for Services to the Crown
Matthew Prenter MCE (Medincross Ltd),
for Services to the Crown

The following are created Copeman Life Peers:
The Lord Wolfe
The Lord Leigh
The Lord Brocket
The Lord Archer

Further Awards are made as follows:
All Members of the Copeman Royal Family
are awarded the Star of Long-Suffering.
Mr Glen Eccles is awarded the Cross of Patience (1st Class).
Colonel Sanders is awarded the Gastronomic Gallantry Medal,
and promoted to Major General with immediate effect.

New Year's Honours will be announced on the
Official King Nicholas Website at www.kingnicholas.com

1

A King is Born

They all were looking for a king
To slay their foes, and lift them high;
Thou cam'st, a little baby thing,
That made a woman cry.
GEORGE MACDONALD (1824–1905)

our Majesty, you must flee now while you still can.'

'I didn't ask for your advice, Archbishop.'

'But Your Majesty, your front lines are breached, the Queen is slain and your own safety is more in doubt the longer you stay.'

'And what qualifies you to advise on matters of war, Archbishop? A mere member of the clergy? Even your own bishops have deserted you in your hour of need. If I were you, I would pray for my life.'

'But I pray only for your life, Your Majesty. Your castle now offers you little protection. If you do not leave now, you face certain death. God save the King!'

'Stop talking like a tit, Baby Face, and move your Irn-Bru out the way – my rook's about to kick your bishop's ass.'

When most people have a game of chess, they just get the board out and play. But that's just not good enough for my best mate John 'Baby Face' Painter who, ever since we were kids, has always insisted that we dress up like wizards, talk in an old-fashioned way and quaff our drinks from tin goblets.

The reason Baby Face was calling me 'Your Majesty' that evening was because earlier in the day we'd both changed our names. We got the idea from Joe Tomms, one of the local idiots in Sheringham, who'd said that his uncle in Norwich had changed his name to Elvis Presley. We didn't believe him at the time, but while we were surfing the Net using the computer in Sheringham Library, we came across the website for UK Deed Poll Online which did indeed allow you to change your name to anything you fancied for just £29.

We still weren't totally convinced it would work, so we tapped in Baby Face's dad's credit card details and each entered a new name – the sillier the better. I was a little shocked when, at the click of a button, the name I'd had for the last twenty-five years was officially changed, from Nicholas Henry John Copeman, to Henry Michael King Nicholas. He changed his from John Kenneth Painter to the Right Reverand Baby Face Archbishop of Fantaberry, solely because he was drinking a bottle of Fanta, which the Head Librarian, Rose Williamson, confiscated, saying, 'Three things are banned in my library: food, drink and superglue.'

Baby Face was annoyed when he came to print out his

details, because there was a red squiggle under the word Reverand, and I pointed out that that was because he'd spelt it incorrectly. After a caution from Rose for swearing, he went back to the website to fork out yet another £29 to correct the error, but then found that he'd have to wait seven days before he could change it again.

A few days later, we received our new National Insurance cards in the post. His said 'TRRBFABO FANTABERRY', which looked stupid, but mine was great … 'HM KING NICHOLAS'.

I don't know why I chose to be called HM King Nicholas. In fact it was actually my second choice after one that referred to female genitalia, which the site rejected. I suppose I just thought it'd be cool to be a king. And my mum's friends at the Salvation Army have always said I look a bit like Prince William.

So though I may have been unemployed and living in a small bungalow in a sleepy Norfolk seaside town, with my mum (Mumsy), dad (Huffa Puffa – so named because of the 'huffa' and 'puffa' noises he makes when he is annoyed by something, usually the 'youth of today') and our dog (Honey), I was now, albeit slightly fraudulently, the king of all I surveyed.

There was something about being called King Nicholas that slowly started to have an effect on me. Nothing drastic to begin with, just little things, such as sitting up straighter when I was watching TV, maybe using a little dish for my crisps instead of eating them straight out of the bag, and occasionally serving my Irn-Bru in one of HP's cocktail glasses, garnished with a maraschino cherry on a stick, instead of slurping it straight out of the can, which Mumsy has always said is unhygienic. I started making an effort to talk in a more refined way too, occasionally saying 'we' instead of 'I', and 'ourself' instead of 'myself', just like the Queen does.

Mumsy seemed generally impressed with my new name, and in particular with the sophisticated manner that came with it. HP said over dinner that he wasn't at all amused and couldn't believe I'd wasted almost a week's benefit money on a new name. He told me to change it back and asked what was wrong with our own family name.

I'm not sure why Baby Face and I wasted so much time doing pointless things like changing our names, but when you haven't got a job and you're living in a town where life goes past at the speed of a shop mobility electric scooter, I suppose you have to make your own entertainment. There are so many 'codger carts' in Sheringham that I once witnessed a pile-up of three of them outside Budgens, resulting in an unlikely case of pavement rage. One old bloke started smacking another on the head with an In-Store Bakery Pain Rustique, while shouting 'heffalump' at him.

By my own standards, Baby Face's lifestyle was rather aspirational. Despite falling out with his parents over a serious matter that he won't tell anyone about, he ended up with his own static caravan on Beeston Regis Caravan Park and got around in a Reliant Scimitar, just like the one Princess Anne drove in the Seventies. Though we were both on the dole, we certainly weren't short of things to do. On the contrary, our Filofaxes were crammed with enough activities to make any head of state need a good power nap.

Most mornings at nine, I'd call on Baby Face and we'd walk at a businesslike pace over to Roy Boy's Truck Stop on the A148 for a Breakfast 'Gut Buster', two cups of tea and a read of the morning papers. Baby Face says you need to keep abreast of current affairs, though he's usually to be found with his head in the *Daily Sport*. On Mondays, we'd get the bus over to the Cromer Job Centre to sign on, then head round to Nobby's Discount Store in Sheringham to buy our groceries for the week: mainly bread, noodles, Irn-Bru, Transform-a-Snacks and Birdseye fish fingers. If it wasn't a Monday, we'd head round to my place to catch *Zena: Warrior Princess* (our house is one of the few in Sheringham that receives Channel 5).

At 10.30 – weather permitting – we'd have a round of putting by the station. In winter we'd revert to Connect 4. At lunchtime we'd have a Pot Noodle and watch *Neighbours* and *Home and Away*. Between 2.00 and 3.30 we'd write letters, and at 4.00 it was afternoon tea at the Salvation Army Drop-In Centre. After tea and cake, we'd rush over to Baby Face's caravan and don our charity shop blazers and ties in time for *Countdown*, have fish fingers or a ready-meal for dinner at six, then a quick game of Fifa on the X-Box before evening television commenced. Sorry to make a boring list of our activities, but I just didn't want you to think we were like all those other people on the dole, who see it as an excuse not to do anything constructive with their time.

The main downside to being on the dole is that there is something of a stigma about it. As I commented to Mr Hill, proprietor of Bertram Watts Booksellers of Sheringham, there are, surprisingly, no style magazines catering for this large market segment. When I mentioned this to Baby Face, he drafted me a letter to the Prince's Trust, which I signed and sent off, outlining our desire to launch a monthly glossy magazine called *People of Leisure*, aimed specifically at those out of work and covering relevant and interesting topics such as managing debt, dressing for success on a budget, and a special colour pull-out section containing snooker and darts tips from the professionals.

Just below my King Nicholas signature, which I'd practised several times on an empty box of Rice Krispies to give it an effortlessly regal appearance, I wrote, 'P.S. We royals should work together – call me if you'd like to meet for tea.'

We received a big envelope in the post the following week containing an information pack and a covering letter from Prince Charles, thanking us for sending in our idea and asking whether we'd like to attend a workshop in Norwich, where we could discuss our business plan further with volunteers from the local business community. Baby Face wetted his finger with a bit of spit and rubbed the signature, which didn't smudge because it was in fact printed on rather than handwritten. Baby Face reckoned that if Prince Charles couldn't be bothered to sign the invitation himself, it probably wasn't worth going along anyway. Entrepreneurs like Baby Face and I are always having great ideas and Baby Face said we couldn't be wasting valuable time and money on train rides into Norwich in response to every letter we received.

As someone very intelligent once said, 'Getting a job is a full-time job in itself', and this is what I kept telling HP, though he seemed totally unconvinced. He kept telling me time and again how, when he was made redundant from his first job in the maize-based snack industry, he didn't just sit around feeling sorry for himself, but rather applied for every single job going – from the Harbour Master at Lowestoft to the newsreader for *Look East*. He did actually end up doing some newsreading for a few months on local TV and became quite a celebrity, culminating in his being asked to officially open the Pound Stretcher in North Walsham. In between writing his job applications, he'd do lots of other useful things, like making concrete doorstops and babies.

All the family have concrete doorstops, embedded with flint

stones and a metal hook in the top, which HP made during this jobless phase. He even made five spare ones to pass on to future generations, so if my sister Clare or I ever have kids, we know what to expect, along with all the other christening presents. Every time my Uncle Peter walks through the side door – we only use the front one for special visitors, such as the Captain of the Salvation Army – he stops and reminds us that it'd be illegal to make a flint doorstop these days because it's an offence to remove beach material. When he says this, he always shakes his head and puts on a very serious look, which a policeman would reserve only for the most serious incidents, such as a driver being twenty times over the limit. Uncle P tends to be very serious about most things, so we tend not to take too much notice. And I was conceived while HP was on the dole – something he blames on 'the long afternoons at home'.

I don't class myself as a dropout, it's just that I think I'm one of those people who need to ease themselves into life gently, a bit like mountaineers who have to acclimatise themselves to altitude gradually before they can ascend a really big mountain. Part of the problem I have is being measured against the success of my older sister, Clare, who has paved the way as far as excellence is concerned. When she was breezing through her 11+ exam and being offered scholarships at lots of posh schools, I was still struggling to read (fair enough I suppose, seeing as I was four), but when she was getting straight As in six A levels, I was still struggling to read and about to fail my 11+. Then, when she was qualifying as an accountant at Ernst & Young in London and busy deciding which colour BMW would work best with her skin tone, I was being advised to downgrade my A levels to AS levels, to give me a better chance of passing at least one.

My sister is very cool and I love her to bits, but I just wish she could have been totally thick, so that I might have won more praise for my own little successes. I am still rather hurt that I received no praise from HP when I won 'chubby bunnies' on a holiday camp (it's that game where you stick as many marsh-mallows as possible into your mouth and try to say 'chubby bunnies'), and all because Clare had done something boring, like getting a place at Cambridge University.

Luckily, I have always been Mumsy's hero. Mumsy's little soldier can do no wrong. After two months of being unem-ployed, I came back from the Job Centre, having been told I'd been put on Job Seekers Plus, which is for people who are doing particularly badly at finding a job. Mumsy thought that the 'Plus' meant I'd been promoted, and she baked a chocolate cake to celebrate. She went round town telling everyone how great I was and Ethel from the charity shop telephoned to congratulate me. Mumsy even phoned Clare to tell her the good news, who told Mumsy that she had herself been promoted, to the board of her firm of accountants. Mumsy said she was very proud of both of her clever children and would post half the chocolate cake to Clare. She iced 'Well Done Cla' on the top, before running out of space. So she had to take the chunk that HP was about to scoff back off him, and reattach it to the end with a smear of leftover chocolate coating that I was planning to spread on some hot pitta bread during one of the commercial breaks in *The Bill*. She then added 'are' by accident so it spelt 'Claare'. Clare called to thank her for the cake a couple of days later, saying it had got a bit squashed in the post, but tasted very nice.

HP, on the other hand, was starting to lose patience with me and thought I needed a bit of military discipline. I'd been a keen member of the Combined Cadet Force at school, where young boys get to smear dirt on their faces and fire machine guns, but I'd dropped out in the sixth form in order to grow long hair and play the drums in a band. HP was one of the last people to do National Service and managed to get a commission in the Royal Navy, just like my Uncle Christopher, whom we all call 'The Commander'. HP thought a stint in the Navy was just what I needed – the perfect experience to make a man of me and instil a sense of pride and discipline. At 25 I would be just young enough to attend selection at the Admiralty Interview Board (AIB) and, if I passed, could go on to get a commission and do quite nicely for myself, money-wise.

Though I lived on the coast, I didn't know much about the Navy, except that it was like the army at sea – they had ships, beards and, someone suggested, they were possibly a bit gay. HP was determined to get me swotted up on what they really did and on current affairs in general, so that I could get a good test score at the AIB. To try and get me excited about his geography and history tutorials, held every evening between five and six, he nicknamed them 'Around the World in Eighty Days'.

My uncle, 'The Commander', is now in his seventies – still a bachelor though – and he served for several years, most of them spent drinking pink gin in the wardroom and typing up orders on a Remington typewriter, though he somehow still managed to get two medals. His favourite toast, used every day as the sun comes over the yardarm: 'Wives and sweethearts … may they never meet.'

The Commander comes round for roast lunch at the bunga-low every other Sunday, catching the Bittern Line train from Norwich and sucking a lozenge so that 'germs might not alight in my oesophagus'. There's always an hour to kill between him arriving and Mumsy and HP getting back from the Salvation

Army service, so HP encouraged him to give me coaching on naval culture. The Commander showed little interest and instead gave me lots of coaching in the types of drinks popular in the Navy and how they were best served and consumed. This, he told me, required a lot of practice, and that it was important that I make him several pink gins to ensure I got into the habit of putting in the right amount of Angostura bitters. The only cocktails I'd heard of before were called things like Slippery Nipple and Sex on the Beach. The Commander scoffed and said on no account to request such drinks in the wardroom, as anything not in the Savoy Cocktail Guide could lead to embarrassment and was almost certainly 'tart fuel'.

In between drinks, he showed me some other stuff, like how to do sword drill, which he started off showing me with a walking stick, until he appeared the following week with the real thing – his Wilkinson ceremonial sword, made by the same people that make the razors. He also showed me how to draw a pistol. He still had the shoulder holster he was issued in Cyprus and had a deactivated Webley to go in it. He claims it's deactivated – I'm not convinced. Mumsy told me off for doing sword drill in the kitchen, because I left lots of little holes in the lino floor where I'd been standing at ease with the point on the ground, and HP was worried that the extension ceiling might spring a leak after I bodged a hole in it doing a salute, where you thrust the blade up in to the air and kiss the handle of the sword. So sword drill was banned from the house, and only to be practised in the garden when Honey was safely indoors.

Name	HM KING NICHOLAS

The types of job I am looking for		SOC
	MANAGING DIRECTOR	1134
	PILOT	3542
		0

I am willing and able to start work
- ⃝ immediately
- ⃝ within 24 hours
- ⃝ within 48 hours
- ◉ other
- ⃝ after giving a weeks notice

I want to limit the days and hours I am available for work
- ⃝ No
- ◉ Yes

I am available for work these days and these hours

	Earliest start time	Latest finish time	Most hours I can work
Monday	—	—	0
Tuesday	—	—	0
Wednesday	12 00	1300	1
Thursday	1200	1300	1
Friday	11 00	1200	1
Saturday	—	—	0
Sunday	—	—	0
Most hours I can work each week			3

2

Work Fit for a King

At night returning, every labour sped,
He sits him down the monarch of a shed.

OLIVER GOLDSMITH (1728–1774)

 don't know what Queen Elizabeth's CV looks like. A bit empty probably:

HM QUEEN ELIZABETH II – CURRICULUM VITAE

Nationality: British
Born: 21st April 1926
Marital status: Married, with four children

Personal Summary:
We are an energetic person and a confident leader, with extensive experience of issuing orders. We are also an excellent communicator and a leading authority on the Queen's English.

Work history:
1952 – Present: Monarch, United Kingdom and Commonwealth. Duties include cutting ribbons, declaring things open and asking subjects if they've come far and enjoy what they do.

Interests:
Shooting, drinking, walking corgis.

Referees:
1. HRH Prince Philip, the Duke of Edinburgh, Buckingham Palace, SW1 1AA
2. Gladys Montphillips, Chief Keeper of the Royal Hounds, Balmoral Castle, Aberdeenshire, AB35 5TB

I wonder what'd happen if she had to get a regular job, like working in Matella or delivering papers for Starlings? Or maybe she could do one of those *Back to the Floor* fly-on-the-wall programmes, where she'd have to go and muck in with the maids at the Palace. I, too, was now a monarch, and also suffering on the CV front. And without the benefit of a civil list, things were a bit tough. Mumsy wasn't at all keen that I should end up in the Navy, because she thought I might get bullied. She wanted me to stay at home where I'd be safe and get proper meals, but like HP, she agreed that I had to get a job, to help contribute to the housekeeping. In a burst of industry she went on a blitz around Sheringham, sorting me out with as many interviews as possible. HP said that if I was going to be taken seriously, I'd need to start dressing properly. My interview suit at the time was an ill-fitting, double-breasted nylon thing that Mumsy bought me in C&A when I was fifteen. It was a horrid, shiny petrol blue, and looked like the sort of thing Uday Hussein would wear. So, at some expense HP sent me to see Mr Green the tailor, to get measured for a bespoke suit because 'nothing suits like a suitable suit'.

Mr Green used to work on Savile Row, but retired to Sheringham fifteen years ago and lives with his wife in 'The Greenhouse', which is actually a small flat above the Co-op. He's in his eighties, but still has a handshake like a vice, and perfect eyesight, which has allowed him to carry on working, mainly doing alterations for Hunt's, the gentleman's outfitters opposite the Little Theatre, which has lots of signs outside saying that anyone caught skateboarding on the marble steps will be shot.

After being measured and attending two subsequent fittings, which were a couple of weeks apart, my suit was finished, just in time for my first interview with the Royal Navy Careers Liaison Officer in London. The transformation was amazing. I'd arrived at Mr Green's lanky and hunched, but left that day with an athletic, V-shaped torso.

Mumsy had arranged for me to have an interview with Dave No Surname, who owns Dave's Fish Bar. I suppose I looked a bit of a plonker being shown around the deep fat fryers and the battering area, wearing such a posh suit. In fact, Dave said he probably wouldn't be needing anyone until late spring anyway, but he gave me a free cod and chips all the same, which would have been very nice had I not dripped tomato sauce on the front of my new jacket.

My next interview was at Blyth & Wright Ironmongers with Ron Wright, who knew my late Uncle Tom (hearth size 17 inches) and had been asked by Mumsy (hearth size 16 inches) whether he might be able to give me a job in the shop. Ron can remember the size of every hearth he's ever fitted in the town. When Mumsy and HP went in to get a new hearth from him, they gave him the address and Ron said, 'Ah, the late Miss Danvers's bungalow: 16 inches.'

All I wanted was a casual job to tide me over till I got something I felt passionate about, like becoming a snack food taste tester, but Ron insisted that if I were to be offered a job with him I'd have to make a lifetime commitment to the firm, because it'd take at least two years for me to learn where everything was and how he liked things to be done. I said I'd have a good think about it and get back to him within six months. I figured it was only right that I take my time over what would be a lifetime commitment. HP agreed that working at Blyth & Wright would make a reasonable back-up option and that if my prospects with the Navy sank without trace, all would not be lost. He said this twice, because he thought it was very funny.

Baby Face surprised me by saying he'd been applying for jobs too, though he was aiming much higher, responding to adverts in *The Times* 'Crème' job section. 'You'll certainly crème yourself when you see the salaries on offer,' he told me. He applied for the Chief Executive position at British Airways saying he had plenty of experience with the company (having flown with them twice in the past) and board director experience (he was the finance director of our Young Enterprise company at school, which was in fact the only one in the history of the scheme to go into liquidation). He got a very pleasant response, thanking him very much for taking the time to apply, saying that they had received many applications in response to the advert, that unfortunately he had been unsuccessful on this occasion, but that they would be keeping his details on file and would notify him should any further executive positions become available to which he might be suited. Baby Face said that, though he might have been pipped to the post for the top job this time round, he felt there was a good chance he'd be offered some other management position in the company, and he could work his way up to CEO in a few years anyway.

Baby Face took the piss out of my new suit and said I looked like 'Tory Boy' off Harry Enfield and that I should get myself a big blue rosette and a load of spots. He went on and on about this all evening and became very irritating. I told him that HP put much of his success in the maize-based snack industry down to the gravitas afforded him by a well-cut blue suit, and that I was planning on making a fair few achievements of my own in mine. I then got up and left without another word, displaying the sort of dignity you'd expect from a king.

3

Emperor's New Clothes

And I looked, and behold, a white horse.
And he who sat on it had a bow; and a crown was given to him,
and he went out conquering and to conquer.

(REVELATION VI:2)

ater that week, I went down to London for my initial interview with the Royal Navy Careers Liaison Officer. It was quite exciting – my last visit to London being when I was ten and Mumsy took me to Hamley's. As I had a bit of time to kill before the interview, I stopped by Buckingham Palace. While it is obviously a lot bigger than our bungalow in Sheringham, I couldn't help thinking that, although it was undoubtedly very impressive, it couldn't be quite as snug and cosy as our home and, though it is very close to a couple of public parks, it does have a rather ugly-looking tarmac forecourt. Mumsy takes pride in keeping our front garden looking nice, maintaining a pleasant view from the sitting room, with the ugly house over the road blocked from sight by strategically placed fence panels, which HP has painted green so they blend in.

My interview was in the heart of Knightsbridge, a pretty posh part of London, with footmen in funny hats and coats standing by doorways and streets lined with the sorts of cars I'd only ever seen in *Top Gear* magazine and at the Great Yarmouth Car Show.

I felt a bit like James Bond as I rang the brass bell next to the unmarked door of a large white building in Iverna Gardens, checking my tie was straight, before being welcomed in by a Royal Marine in khaki uniform. I wiped my feet on the large 'Royal Navy' doormat and followed him through the main building, then out through a big hole in the back wall into a warehouse where I was welcomed by a young officer called Lieutenant Chiverst, who was wearing slacks and a tweed jacket and spoke a bit like 'Q'.

The way HP and the Commander went on about the Navy, they gave the impression it was all to do with battleships and killing people, so I was pleasantly surprised to find from the brochures and videos that Lieutenant Chiverst showed me in a little interview room in the warehouse that it was much more to do with skiing, swimming, sunbathing and general camaraderie. We had a good chat about the price of drinks in the wardroom and the sorts of ceremonial uniforms officers wear, and Lieutenant Chiverst, in passing, commented favourably on my suit.

He said I was just the sort of chap the Royal Navy was after and that he was going to put my name forward for the next Admiralty Interview Board. He also said that, at the age of 25, if

I did get selected for the Royal Naval College I'd receive an automatic promotion to sub-lieutenant upon entry, which I really liked the sound of. It would mean I'd get paid extra and, perhaps more importantly, I'd get to wear smart gold bands on my uniform sleeves instead of silly little white patches on my collar.

The following morning back in Sheringham, I went round to see Baby Face, to show him the information pack I'd been given and to show off some of my expert swordsmanship. Baby Face was most impressed, with the Commander's naval sword in particular. He pointed out, quite rightly, that several members of the British Royal Family had served in the Royal Navy, so it could be quite a good career move for me too, what with being a king and all.

Baby Face told me that while I'd been down in London, he'd been developing his own persona and had got together some archbishop's clothes. During the commercial break in *Who Wants to be a Millionaire?* he popped into his bedroom, re-emerging a few moments later wearing a white nightie, a red scarf, and a tea cosy on his head. When I called it a tea cosy, he looked quite offended, and told me it was a mitre. He'd been talking to Uncle P about what he should wear as an archbishop. Uncle P's a guide at Norwich Cathedral and he'd told Baby Face that the mitre symbolises the cloven tongues of fire which descended on the apostles on the day of Pentecost. Baby Face had duly cut out a big piece of card in the shape of a tongue, painted it pink and stapled it to the top of the tea cosy, along with a slightly wonky cross, which he'd glued to the front. As for the nightie, Baby Face told me it was actually a 'chasuble', which he'd swapped for five two-litre bottles of Tizer with Andrew Cartmell, who's a chorister at

St Peter's Church. I asked him what the official name for his scarf was. He said it *was* a scarf. I nodded appreciatively and told him it was a very smart costume indeed. It wasn't really all that good – I was just being polite – and I did hint that five bottles of Tizer seemed rather a lot to pay for something he'd only wear around the caravan. After all, it wasn't as if he'd dare wear it in public.

Using the word 'dare' was a bad move. In fact, I knew I'd made a mistake the moment I said it. If you ask me, 'dare' is quite possibly the most loaded word in the English dictionary and to say 'You wouldn't dare' or 'I dare you' is probably the ultimate challenge of a gentleman's mettle, rattling something at his very core – a kind of chivalrous code of conduct stemming back to his days in the playground, when dared to climb a wall, steal some sweets or pinch Katy Wilmott. Baby Face looked surprised and perhaps a little bit hurt that I'd challenged him in this way and asked whether he'd heard me correctly.

Baby Face insisted he'd have absolutely no problem going out in public in his new clothes – in fact he'd do it without thinking twice and certainly didn't need to be dared. Not like me, on the other hand, who he said didn't have the balls to do anything adventurous without a good kick up the arse. He pointed out that I was as much a king as he was an archbishop, but that when it came down to it I would never be more than a king in name, because I didn't have the guts of a real figurehead, who'd be out there doing king-type stuff to justify their place on the list on the back of people's wooden rulers, rather than just sitting in a caravan watching *Who Wants to be a Millionaire?*.

I was quite offended. While I might have changed my name to King Nicholas just for fun, I thought it very rude and quite untrue of him to say that I couldn't live up to the title. I felt that I was far more convincing as a king than he was as an archbishop.

The conversation got quite heated – so much so that we carried on bickering throughout the second part of *Who Wants to be a Millionaire?* and didn't even notice when it got to a question for a quarter of a million pounds. Baby Face said that if I was, as I claimed, a *real* king, then there was only one way to prove it – by going out and showing everyone. Like people who get married, confirmed or turn gay.

We were due at the Job Centre on Monday morning, and Baby Face reckoned that'd be the perfect opportunity to show the world I was King. He said he'd had enough of shuffling in there every week, feeling like a second-class citizen, and that it was time to put the pizzazz back into unemployment. He said he'd be going dressed as the Archbishop, and if I had even an ounce of respect for myself, I'd turn up as the King. Unless of course I was chicken, and no one likes a chicken unless it's a KFC.

Back at the bungalow, I was telling Mumsy about Baby Face's mad idea. I was hoping for a bit of level-headed support but, rather than agreeing with me, she said it sounded like a lovely idea and why was I being such a spoilsport? She said she could have me looking the part in no time and, after she'd put a load of scones in the oven, she went off to the spare room. She came back a few minutes later with a heap of fabric, a metal tin and a battered old box with my gran's writing on the side. The tin was full of buttons, of assorted sizes and colours, and the box, which I recognised well, contained a brass advent crown, which has red hearts painted all around it and holders for four candles, which we light – an extra one each week – every Sunday during the run-up to Christmas.

Mumsy reckoned she'd have just enough velour material to make me a rather snazzy cloak, though it'd have to be done in two different colours, because she didn't have enough of either colour to make the whole thing. I was only half listening to her because my attention was fixed on the crown, which was sitting in the box on top of its red velvet plinth. It had been in the family ever since I could remember, and I'd always thought of it as just a candle-holder. But looking at it now, without its candles in, it did look just like a crown – it was an 'advent crown' after all.

I didn't want Mumsy to see me try it on because I'd feel really silly, so, while she was setting up her sewing machine, I took it out of the box and sneaked out into the utility room and stood in front of the little mirror by the back door. I slowly lowered the crown onto my head and, as I did so and for no apparent reason, I suddenly felt a shiver down my spine. Apart from the spiky legs, which dug into my head a bit, it was a perfect fit. And I didn't look all that silly either. In fact I looked just like a king and I couldn't help thinking of the old saying, 'If the cap fits – wear it.'

I went back into the kitchen and put the crown in the box. Mumsy had started sewing away, and she finished making me a cloak later that evening, with big medieval-looking buttons down the front, which looked like the sort of thing Tony Robinson would dig up on *Time Team*, but which were actually made of moulded plastic. Next morning, I was a bit miffed to find that my favourite jogging bottoms had come back from the wash with gold braid sewn down the seams and that my Green Flash trainers now had big gold bows with little bells on them stuck to the toes.

I would have felt awkward enough parading around in a proper costume from the BBC Props Department, but in this clobber I was just going to look like a total tosser. Still, I didn't want to offend Mumsy, who'd put in a lot of work, so I pretended I thought my new outfit was absolutely wonderful.

On Monday morning, just after nine, I walked round to Baby Face's caravan, carrying my new costume in a black bin bag. I arrived to find two horses tethered up outside. Baby Face has been into riding ever since he was a kid. His dad bought him his own horse several years back. It's a bit old now and won't gallop any more, but is still fine for popping down the shops on, or for using to get back from the pub when Baby Face is over the limit. And of course horses don't use petrol, which Baby Face says is great, because his Scimitar gets through a hell of a lot as it's got a V6 engine. Baby Face couldn't afford the upkeep on his horse any more, so he'd started to let the stables use it for teaching lessons, in exchange for free board (for the horse, not him).

I knocked on the side of his van and he came to the door, wearing nothing but his Y-fronts and mitre – I was hoping he might have forgotten about the dare, but clearly he hadn't. Inside, he told me how he'd done a dress-rehearsal the previous evening at St Peter's Church, where he'd taken it upon himself to stand outside the main door and welcome the congregation as they came in for the service. Apparently, the vicar looked a bit blank later on when one of the women from the choir told him what a nice young man the new curate was.

Baby Face was eager to see my new costume so, reluctantly, I used his bedroom to get changed into my kit, while he put the kettle on. When I came back in, he insisted I do a twirl. He was particularly impressed by my crown, which now had gaffer tape wrapped round the legs, so they didn't dig into my head.

As we drank our tea and dunked away with some Bourbon biscuits, Baby Face asked whether I'd seen my new wheels outside. He was referring to the white horse, which he told me was called 'Noel Edmonds', and which he'd borrowed from the stables, so I could ride over to the Job Centre with him in fitting style.

I wasn't impressed. As Baby Face knows, I'm scared of horses. I just can't get my head round a form of transport that craps, snorts and, on occasion, buckaroos, just like the plastic donkey on the game we still play. Baby Face said that Noel Edmonds was very well behaved and would never buckaroo – in fact, he was an ex-police horse, so you could ride him through a riot without him getting at all agitated. I wasn't convinced – on the few occasions I'd ridden a horse I got very nervous, and always insisted on riding side-saddle to make it easier to jump off should it decide to bolt.

Baby Face said we'd better get a move on if we were going to get over to the Job Centre for 10.30 – after all, it'd take longer to get there by horse than it did by bus. He put on his fleece jacket and threw his chasuble over the top, then we headed out into the brisk autumn air. I wished my crown had a velvet bit inside it at the top, like the Queen's, instead of being open-topped, which made my head a bit cold. Baby Face gave me a leg up onto my horse and we headed off down the coastal path. I had to lay my sword across my lap to stop it banging against my ankle as I rode along. Baby Face was carrying a nice new shepherd's crook, which he said he'd 'borrowed' from the wall of the Dunstable Arms.

What surprised me was that any sense of embarrassment started to evaporate as we rode along the clifftops, like two ancient noblemen from a time long past. It was only when we passed a few dog walkers near East Runton that I felt a bit self-conscious and quickly hid my crown under my cloak. I suppose Orlando Bloom must have had to deal with the same feeling when he played Legolas in *The Lord of the Rings*, and had to wear a funny costume and wig and try and remain serious in front of that hairy director and the rest of the film crew, who'd all have been wearing jeans and baseball caps and chewing gum. So I did my best to put any feelings of silliness to the back of my mind and just concentrate on getting the dare over with.

When we arrived in Cromer, we couldn't agree where to leave the horses while we went to sign on. I wanted to leave them in the Pay and Display, but Baby Face said there was no way he was paying sixty pence to park his horse up, and that we'd try and find a space somewhere nearer the Job Centre, so we could keep an eye on them. We found a drainpipe right outside, which Baby Face tethered them up to, and he then bent over at the side of Noel Edmonds so I could dismount by stepping down onto his shoulder. I accidentally jabbed him in the arm with my sword sheath in the process, which made him scream loudly. This startled Noel Edmonds, who Baby Face had assured me was unstartleable, and I ended up in a very undignified position, with my foot trapped in the stirrup and my legs spread wide apart. It took Baby Face a couple of minutes, and the help of a passer-by, to free me, and by then a small crowd had gathered around us to see what all the commotion was about. I tried hard to maintain my Orlando Bloom focus, but I couldn't help feeling like a total idiot.

But a dare was a dare, and the only thing worse than doing this would be not doing it, and then being subjected to the ridicule of Baby Face for ever more. So I took a moment to compose myself and straighten my cloak before I swung open the door to the Job Centre and strode in, advent crown à tête, to discuss my suitability for a job in a pie packing factory.

My employment officer, Jane Harley, didn't seem at all impressed with me, or with Baby Face, who was hovering around in the background, and making a nuisance of himself by blessing the people that were looking at the job cards in the window. To add to the distraction, Noel Edmonds started to get bothered by the passing traffic outside, and kept banging his hooves on the pavement and bumping against the Job Centre window. I apologised to Jane and said I'd better go and check he was all right. Jane was very angry and said that if I wasn't going to take my search for a job seriously, my situation would have to be reviewed, 'with possible financial repercussions'.

I was lucky to get my benefit that week. Jane didn't really believe my story, that we were dressed up because we were off to a fancy dress party later, and she only signed my form once I'd shovelled up all the fresh manure off the pavement outside, using a small plastic bucket and spade that I had to buy from the one-pound shop over the road.

On the way back to Baby Face's caravan, Noel Edmonds kept veering about without warning and, once we'd got back more or less safely, Baby Face confessed that he wasn't really an ex-police horse. He'd just made it up so I'd agree to ride along with him.

4

Coronation Chicken

Baby Face the priest and Zinger the prophet
anointed Nicholas King.

I KINGS, I:39

'Two Zinger Tower Burgers please.'
'Meals or just the burgers?'
'Just the burgers please.'
'£5.30.'

I always go down KFC when there's big business to do. Today it was my coronation.

Apparently there's a book about how fast food is full of crap. But if you've ever smelt a Zinger Tower Burger, all that goes out the window. I'm not being paid to plug KFC here ... the Zinger

Tower truly is a gastronomic masterpiece. One day, I will open an expensive restaurant next door to a KFC. No swanky wanky food will be served though, I'll get the chef to pop next door and buy Zinger Towers, then serve them on big white plates, drizzled with Zinger sauce, for twenty pounds a pop.

The burgers were for me and Baby Face – our pre-coronation lunch. Baby Face had his archbishop's costume packed away in his rucksack because I kept complaining when he wore it out in public. As far as I was concerned, I'd done my bit by going into the Job Centre in costume and was in no hurry to wear it again. I bet Batman and Robin must have had the piss taken out of them when they were out and about in costume – maybe they only started wearing capes and Day-Glo underpants for a dare too. At least they had masks to conceal their identity, so that none of the locals would know it was actually them. I suppose Baby Face and I were a 'dynamic duo' of sorts – me being the superhero king in the velour cape, and him being the capable – though slightly less dynamic and handsome – sidekick.

Baby Face was taking his role as Archbishop increasingly seriously and had even made enquiries about getting his 'Zinger Religion' made official. Apparently, in the census one year, several thousand people had put down 'Jedi' as their religion and it was made an officially recognised faith as a result. One day, he came rushing round to the bungalow, clutching a printout from a website he'd just signed up to. I was amazed.

BE ORDAINED NOW!

Become a legally ordained minister within 48 hours
As a minister, you will be authorized to perform the rites and ceremonies of the church!

Perform Weddings, Funerals, and Perform Baptisms Forgiveness of Sins and Visit Correctional Facilities

Want to open a church?
Check out Ministry in a Box...

Minister Charles Simpson has the power to make you a LEGALLY ORDAINED MINISTER within 48 hours!!!

WEDDINGS
- MARRY your BROTHER, SISTER, or your BEST FRIEND!!
- Don't settle for being the BEST MAN OR BRIDES' MAID
- Most states require that you register your certificate (THAT WE SEND YOU) with the state prior to conducting the ceremony.

FUNERALS
- A very hard time for you and your family
- Don't settle for a minister you don't know!!
- Most states require that you register your certificate (THAT WE SEND YOU) with the state prior to conducting the ceremony.

BAPTISMS
- You can say 'WELCOME TO THE WORLD!!!! I AM YOUR MINISTER AND YOUR UNCLE!!'
- What a special way to welcome a child of God.

FORGIVENESS OF SINS
- The Catholic Church has practiced the forgiveness of sins for centuries

- Forgiveness of Sins is granted to all who ask in sincerity and willingness to change for the better!!

VISIT CORRECTIONAL FACILITIES
- Since you will be a Certified Minister, you can visit others in need!!
- Preach the Word of God to those who have strayed from the flock

WANT TO START YOUR OWN CHURCH??
- Ministry in a Box!
- After your LEGAL ORDINATION, you may start your own congregation!!

At this point you must be wondering how much the Certificate costs. Right? Well, let's talk about how much the program is worth. Considering the value of becoming a CERTIFIED MINISTER I'd say the program is easily worth $100. Wouldn't you agree? However, it won't cost that much. Not even close! My goal is to make this life-changing program affordable so average folks can benefit from the power of it.

Since I know how much you want to help others, you're going to receive your Minister Certification for under $100.00...

Not even $50.00...

You are going to receive the entire life-changing course for only $29.95.

For only $29.95 you will receive:

1. 8-inch by 10-inch certificate IN COLOR, WITH GOLD SEAL. (CERTIFICATE IS PROFESSIONALLY PRINTED BY AN INK PRESS)
2. Proof of Minister Certification in YOUR NAME!!
3. SHIPPING IS FREE!!!

LIMITED TIME OFFER: ORDER TODAY!

SHIPPING IS FREE!!! For Shipping OUTSIDE the US please add $11.00.
(ALL ORDERS FILLED WITHIN 24 HOURS OF RECEIVING THEM)
● Please allow 8 days to receive your certificate by mail.

PAY BY CREDIT CARD or PAY BY CHECK

Baby Face was eager to try out his new powers, and had prepared a special coronation ceremony for me. He'd even got a black and white badge made for himself at Blyth & Wright, which looked like the sort of thing that those Mormons wear when they do door-to-door visits, and it said 'The Right Reverand Baby Face, Zinger Church'.

As preparation for the ceremony, he'd found out loads of information on past coronations and had come across a particularly useful site called 'The Orange Pages: The Burning Torch for Protestantism', where some nice bloke had written up a full transcript of Queen Elizabeth's coronation.

After we'd finished our Zinger Towers, we climbed on our horses and set off along the coastal path through East Runton, then West Runton, and on to Beeston Bump, the hill overlooking Sheringham and the sea. There I was to be officially crowned King, by following an Order of Service that he'd printed out. Baby Face had strapped a ghettoblaster onto his horse, which he referred to as his car stereo, and was playing his John Miles *Rebel* CD on it, which skipped occasionally as the horse trotted along. I still hadn't got the hang of riding properly and could never quite get in sync with the motion of Noel Edmonds, resulting in an undignified and jolty ride. This was making me feel rather queasy, since my Zinger burger hadn't had time to go down properly, so when we passed nearby Baby Face's caravan in Beeston, I asked him if we could stop for a quick sit down.

At his van, we got a bit side-tracked from the official business of my coronation because *Bargain Hunt* with David Dickinson was on and we can never resist placing bets on the lots. Baby Face then insisted on sticking around to watch *Angry Beavers* on ITV at 3.35 because he'd never seen it before and wondered what it was about. It was a cartoon about two beaver bachelors called Daggett and Norbert. Baby Face was a little disappointed, but said he rather liked the characters and would tune in again next time it was on because he empathised with Daggett, who wanted to become a brain surgeon but didn't want to spend any time studying.

It was getting dark when we finally got back on our horses and made our way up Beeston Bump. When we got to the top, Baby Face jumped off his horse and climbed onto the concrete triangulation pillar. Below us, in the town, the street lights were coming to life and cars were starting to turn on their headlights.

'Sir, is Your Majesty willing to take the Oath?'

'I am willing.'

'Will you solemnly promise and swear to govern your peoples according to prevailing laws and customs?

'I solemnly promise so to do.'

'Will you strive inviolably for the return of the McRib to the regular McDonald's menu?'

'I will.'

'Will you maintain and preserve inviolably the settlement of the Church of Zinger, and the doctrine, worship, discipline and government thereof? And will you preserve unto the Bishops and Clergy, and to the Churches there committed to their charge, all such rights and privileges, as by law do or shall appertain to them or any of them?'

'Em, yeah, I think so.'

Then he took the Commander's sword out of the sheath that I'd strapped to the back of my horse and passed it to me, saying:

Receive this kingly sword,
Brought now from the Altar of Zinger,
And delivered to you by the hands of me
The Bishop and servant of Zinger, though unworthy.
With this sword do justice,
Stop the growth of iniquity,
Protect the holy Church of Zinger,
Help and defend widows and orphans,
Restore the things that are gone to decay,
Maintain the things that are restored,
Punish and reform what is amiss,
And confirm what is in good order:
That doing these things you may be glorious in all virtue;
And so faithfully serve our Lord Zinger in this life,
That you may reign for ever with him

In the life which is to come.
Amen.

Baby Face held out an empty Zinger Tower Burger box and invited me to place my right hand on it.

'There's a load of other stuff we're supposed to do too,' he said, 'but *Ready Steady Cook* starts in a few minutes and Leslie Ash is on and I want to see if she's still got a trout pout, so just read this sentence at the bottom and we'll call it a day.'

With my hand on the box, I read from the piece of paper Baby Face was holding out.

'The things which I have here promised, I will perform, and keep. So help me God.'

Then Baby Face took the advent crown out of his rucksack and lowered it onto my head.

'God Save the King!' he proclaimed, in a loud though characteristically whiny voice. No one heard him, except me, him, the two horses and maybe the walker in the distance throwing a ball for his dog.

I was hoping to savour the moment, but Baby Face did a loud Zinger burp and jumped straight off the triangulation pillar and back onto his horse. He rummaged around in his rucksack and pulled out another CD. As we rode back down Beeston Bump towards his caravan, the majestic sounds of *Zadok the Priest* blasted out across the fields. It was official. In the eyes of God and, more importantly, the Archbishop of Fantaberry, I was King.

'I wonder what AWT's going to be cooking up today?' asked Baby Face, to no one in particular.

THE NEW KING OF SHERINGHAM?!?!

You might be forgiven for thinking that the last time 'GOD SAVE THE KING!' was proclaimed in England, King George VI was on the throne. Not so! Local lad, Nick Copeman, has shocked the people of Sheringham by proclaiming himself THE KING OF A NEW EMPIRE that he is running with John 'Baby Face' Painter from his caravan in Beeston. John is himself making the bold claim of being ARCHBISHOP!!!

In an exclusive interview with the Sheringham Independent, KING NICHOLAS, as he INSISTS on being called, said, "Elvis was the King, and no one said it was treason. No one has ever turned up at Burger King and told them off either, as far as I know. I have never claimed I'm the King of England anyway. I am the King of the Copeman Empire."

King Nicholas is currently unemployed but says he has MANY AMBITIOUS PLANS for his Empire which he says are, "To remain secret until such time as we see fit to decree."

Talking Point ☞ What do you think about King Nicholas? Should we tolerate eccentric people/anti-social behaviour in our town??? Or, as some persons would say, discourage such 'antisocial behaviour'??? HAVE YOUR SAY..... Write to: The Sheringham Independent, 2a Melbourne Road, NR26 8EF, Tel/Fax 01263 824721, email:sherindie@aol.com, Opening times: Mon & Thu 9.30 -11.30. Deadline for next issue October 16th.

Audrey Jones

15th March 1911 - 29th September 2003

Life is mostly froth and bubble,
Two things stand like stone -
Kindness in another's trouble,
Courage in your own.

(Full obituary on next page)

5

The Fourth Estate

The pen is mightier than the sword.
EDWARD GEORGE EARLE LYTTON BULWER-LYTTON (1803–1873)

don't know why they bother having a local newspaper in Sheringham. It's not like anyone relies on
the press to keep them up to date with what's
happening around town. After all, that's the allot-
ment committee's job – a loyal network of old-age
pensioners, who use their interest in vegetable patches as a
cover for their main role – circulating juicy gossip. They might
all be in their eighties and have more titanium bones than real
ones, but give them a prime titbit of information and they'll
spring into action faster than Daley Thompson, zipping from
door to door, whispering over fences, ringing their friends up
on their Bakelite phones and passing word to Roy Boy, who in

turn passes it on to every local who stops off for a bacon bap. People got very agitated when they heard that I was going round town claiming to be a king, and the consensus among the old-timers was that it was 'treason and blasphemy' claiming to have been anointed by God.

I received a telephone call later that afternoon from Helen, the editor of the *Sheringham Independent*, who said that she'd been tipped off that I'd proclaimed myself King of England and the Son of God, and was this true? I explained that I had proclaimed myself King – not of England but of a new, and far better nation, to be called the Copeman Empire, and that at this stage I was still in the process of coming up with a constitution, so things were all a bit up in the air. As for being the Son of God, this was news to me.

It was obviously a bit of a slow news day because we had quite a long chat, about the pressures of being a king and being unemployed. Helen said that most royals were, in effect, unemployed – a very perceptive observation which I made a note of, for next time HP was giving me a hard time.

HP almost choked on his porridge that Saturday morning, when he opened up the paper to find a half-page story about me on Page 7. I had hoped to be front-page news, but on the night before they went to press, two local hooligans dug up the middle of the green at the Morley Bowls Club with soup ladles. So I appeared alongside an advert for 'The Iron Lady: Professional Ironing Service', and an obituary for Audrey Jones, who had finally died at the age of 92.

THE NEW KING OF SHERINGHAM?!?!

You might be forgiven for thinking that the last time 'GOD SAVE THE KING!' was proclaimed in England, King George

VI was on the throne. Not so! Local lad, Nick Copeman, has shocked the people of Sheringham by proclaiming himself THE KING OF A NEW EMPIRE that he is running with John 'Baby Face' Painter from his caravan in Beeston. John is himself making the bold claim of being ARCHBISHOP!!!

In an exclusive interview with the *Sheringham Independent*, KING NICHOLAS, as he INSISTS on being called, said, 'Elvis was the King, and no one said it was treason. No one has ever turned up at Burger King and told them off either, as far as I know. I have never claimed I'm the King of England anyway. I am the King of the Copeman Empire.'

King Nicholas is currently unemployed but says he has MANY AMBITIOUS PLANS for his Empire which he says are, 'To remain secret until such time as we see fit to decree.'

Talking Point ☞ What do you think about King Nicholas? Should we tolerate eccentric people/anti-social behaviour in our town??? Or, as some persons would say, discourage such 'antisocial behaviour'??? HAVE YOUR SAY... Write to: The Sheringham Independent, 2a Melbourne Road, NR26 8EF, Tel/Fax 824721, email: sherindie@aol.com, Opening times: Mon & Thu 9.30–11.30. Deadline for next issue October 16th.

HP went bonkers. He was embarrassed enough by the article itself, but was particularly annoyed that it appeared right next to the obituary for Audrey Jones, who was a friend of the family and a good friend of the Lord Mayor of Norwich. He paced up and down the kitchen, huffing and puffing about how the Copeman name had been tarnished. HP likes to think the family is highly thought of in the area and he, himself, gained a near-legendary reputation in the maize-based snack industry as the man that backed Phileas Fogg when they were still just a bunch of unknowns up in Consett.

He stomped out of the back door and headed for his shed, probably to eat some pork scratchings, have a swig of brandy and hopefully steer clear of the power tools. While he'd been having a go at me, Mumsy had been quietly reading the article, and once he'd left the room, she said, 'Who'd have thought it? My son ... a king ... and in the paper.' Then she gave me a big hug and a sloppy kiss.

6
Copeman Palace

There was a very stately palace before him,
The name of which was Copeman.
JOHN BUNYAN (1628–1688)

igar smoke swirled around him in a sinister fog. Only the glow of burning leaves and his jewel-like, piercing eyes cut through the charged atmosphere. He tapped a lump of ash onto a plate and his shirtsleeve rode up, revealing a scar on his hand. In front of him was the briefcase. He pushed it across the table towards me.

I rotated the case so that the locks were facing me. There was a scratching sound as I did so, a small piece of grit, perhaps, trapped between the leather of the case and the wood of the table. I looked back at him. He said nothing, just held his steady stare, waiting for me to make a move. I pulled at the catches. They didn't move. I tried again. My thumbs – sweaty – slipped slightly, but the latches stuck fast.

'The case is locked,' he croaked, in a menacing, Italian accent. Raising his cigar to his mouth, the leaves crackled as he inhaled.

'"666" on the left lock. "999" on the right.'

I flipped the case up so that I could see the golden dials in the low light. I slowly ratcheted them into position, then laid the case flat again. I looked at him once more. He remained motionless, like a panther, ready to pounce without warning. I pulled the catches once more and they flicked open with a dull thud.

'Open it,' he said, his voice throaty and worn – a man who'd seen the darker side of life, and lived not to tell the tale. I lifted the lid and locked it into place. And there it was. In neat stacks. I looked at it for a few moments, then ran my fingers over the surface, before picking up a stack and flicking through the notes.

I am very proud of that bit of writing. It's that kind of quality that nearly got me a C in GCSE English. Maybe one day I'll get into proper novel writing like Jeffrey Archer and John Grisham, using my in-depth understanding of the inner workings of the benefit system to deliver a hard-hitting action drama. I might call it *The Runaway Dole Queue*, where people would suddenly, and for no apparent reason, stop going to the Job Centre and they'd trade in their shell suits for Armani ones, and drive around in Porsches and Mercedes, waving loads of cash about. No one would be able to work out why – I haven't even worked it out myself yet – but there'd be a really interesting, semi-believable reason for it that'd get questions asked at the highest level, maybe even at the North Norfolk District Council.

There'd be a clever twist in the tale too, and the reviewers would love it and say:

The Runaway Dole Queue is Copeman at his best: a hard-hitting, nail-biting, high-octane juggernaut of excitement and passion, which keeps the pages turning like a hot kebab that's turning extra-fast and with loads of chilli sauce on it – The Sun

The book Grisham would write, had he Copeman's talent – The Times

You'll never think about shell suits in the same way again. A masterpiece – Daily Telegraph

Baby Face hadn't spoken to his mum and dad in months now and they didn't bother to tell him when his gran, Jane Painter, died. He found out from Roy Boy, who asked him why he was eating a pheasant burger in his lay-by, when the rest of his family was at his gran's funeral. To be honest, Baby Face didn't like his gran much and she certainly didn't like him. In fact I don't think she liked anyone, or anything, except quality biscuits and advocaat. Once, when we were younger, I remember Baby Face and I went round to visit her and she brought out some tea and biscuits for us. She gave us a rich tea biscuit each, but had a plate of Maryland Choc Chip cookies to herself. When Baby Face nabbed one off her plate and dunked it into his mug of tea, she dunked his whole hand into the mug, giving him a nasty scald, which doesn't tan properly to this day.

Apart from the luxury biscuits, Granny Painter led a very humble existence. A spinster all her life, she lived in a small cottage on New Road, which her own gran had bought when it actually was a new road, back in the 1890s. But the Painters had always wondered what they'd find in her will, if she actually had one. As she hated absolutely everyone, it was hard to work out who would get anything.

It turned out she did have a will, which was more like a hate letter than an allocation of assets, going through each family member one by one, undertaking a character assassination, then saying how much he or she had been left. Baby Face didn't attend the reading of the will, but later in the day, he popped into Walter Smith & Co Solicitors, who told him that he was a 'snivelling little prig' and that he'd been left £30,000. Baby Face said he was speechless.

Now, I don't know who you are and what thirty grand might do to your life. Maybe it'd just buy some new custom-made taps for one of the en-suites in your big house, or pay for a year's education for one of your kids. But if you're anything like Baby Face or me, who get less than £50 in benefit a week, plus a few quid for washing cars or selling bits and bobs on the side, the idea of getting thirty grand is about as life changing as a sex change, or so I'd imagine, based on an article I once read in a magazine in the dentist's waiting room.

Baby Face just didn't know what to do with himself. In fact, he decided he might not be doing much for the foreseeable future, and was considering taking early retirement. I asked him whether it was actually possible to retire before he'd even had his first proper job.

As soon as the cheque had cleared, he said he needed to see the money, just to believe it was really there. So he went into HSBC, took out £60, and said that he'd be back for the rest later. He went over to Bertram Watts and bought a leather-look briefcase, then went straight back to the bank to take out the remaining cash. But Adrian, the bank manager, said the maximum daily withdrawal was £200, unless at least twenty-four hours' notice was given in advance. So Baby Face gave his notice, took out another fifty quid, and said he'd be back at the same time tomorrow. Then he went off to Marmalades Bistro for a no-expense-spared, slap-up meal.

ews of Baby Face's new-found wealth was around town in a flash. The next day, when he returned to the bank to collect his fortune, an army of old biddies had gathered to witness the event. As a security precaution, he'd popped into Starlings beforehand and bought a pair of plastic handcuffs from the toy section, which he then used to lock the briefcase to his wrist. It turned out that £30,000 in fifty-pound notes didn't take up as much room in his case as he'd imagined (he'd been hoping for the full-on drugs dealer effect) so he decided to pop over to Nobby's, and bought ten boxes of cream liqueur milk chocolates, which he stuck under the money to bolster it up. Then he visited Scotter's Wet Fish Shop to buy a lobster and dropped into the Crossroads tobacconist to buy a big Romeo & Juliet cigar.

On Sunday evening, he invited me round to his caravan for a celebratory dinner. He was smoking away on his cigar, which made him cough a lot, and he kept putting on a ridiculous Al Pacino voice. That was when he passed me the briefcase and let me look at the money, as I described, so eloquently, earlier on. He said that later, after I'd left, he was planning to throw the money all over his bed and lie on top of it with no clothes on, indulging in a bit of 'hand-to-gland combat', while watching *Scrap Heap Challenge* with Lisa Rogers. Before I left him to it, we had lobster on a bed of Pot Noodles for dinner. We didn't know how to cook a lobster so we just broke it in half with a hammer and boiled it in a pot. In fact, it turned out not too bad, though Baby Face claims it gave him the squits, and we both agreed that posh nosh is rarely all it's cracked up to be.

While we tucked in, Baby Face told me how he planned to invest the money. He said he was going to buy a place to live. He obviously didn't have a clue how much houses in Sheringham cost – thirty grand might have bought you a bungalow twenty years ago, but certainly not now. But then he handed me a well-fingered brochure for Regal Caravans, pointing out the aptness of the name. Each of the models had an impressive name, such as Diplomat, Ambassador, Commissioner and Emperor.

The van that had caught Baby Face's eye was the Ambassador, because it had proper, stand-alone furniture, rather than fitted-in benches and a folding table like those in his current one. Looking at the photos of the interior, it was hard to tell that you weren't looking at a house, and a rather pleasantly appointed one at that. There was even an elegant-looking MDF carriage clock above the fireplace, which I could have sworn was a real coal fire, but which Baby Face assured me was actually run on gas. And to top it all, he said they had a show home version available, which had previously been on display at their main showroom in Lowestoft and was now available at a 15 per cent discount with all sorts of extras fully fitted, but that he had to be quick, because it wouldn't be long before someone snapped it up.

He said that, though he'd obviously be moving into the new van, he wouldn't be getting rid of the old one, because it held too many fond memories. And one day, if he started a family, he might need the extra space. Then he said something very kind.

He said that if I wanted, I could live in his old van. That if I got it cleaned out and tarted up a bit, it'd make a palace fit for a king.

I was going to reject the idea out of hand, like most of his stupid ideas, but then I thought, maybe this could be just what I needed. Maybe this was my chance to strike out on my own, fly the nest, chart my course and stride forth to a bright future of independence and prosperity. And Baby Face had another cunning wheeze. He could charge me rent, which would be paid to him by Housing Benefit on my behalf, but he'd then give half of it straight to me, as a backhander. And by bumping up the rent as high as we could get away with, we might receive as much as £60 each, on top of our benefit every week, and that'd be more than the benefit itself. I told him it was a very generous offer, but that I thought it was dishonest. He said it was simply creative funds management.

HP had often told me how Phileas Fogg built a snack empire from a small Portakabin at the back of the British Steel depot in Consett, and now I had the chance to do the same. Except I wouldn't be making snacks. I'd be making something far more important. I just had to think what it might be.

When I floated the idea at home, they weren't at all happy. HP started huffing and puffing and Mumsy looked very hurt. HP said my mind should be focused on the AIB, and Mumsy said it was getting too cold to be camping out. I explained to her that I wouldn't be camping out – it was a caravan, and had all sorts of creature comforts, including central heating. This made Mumsy feel much better about the whole idea, but still, she insisted that, if I did end up moving out, I take my paisley nightcap with me to keep any draughts out while I was sleeping. And HP said I could only live on my own if I got up at no later than eight o'clock every morning, had *The Times* delivered and still came round for my Navy coaching every night. And of course Honey would still be expecting me to give her her usual walk over Beeston Bump every Wednesday and Sunday morning.

So it was agreed. The Copeman Empire was granted its independence. On 20 October, Baby Face took delivery of his Regal Ambassador. The delivery was rather a palaver because he wanted the new one placed in the exact spot that the current one was in, and the old one – which was soon to become mine – swung through ninety degrees so that the two vans would form a right angle around an enclosed area, which he planned to have decked, like he'd seen on *Ground Force*. So the flatbed lorry that delivered the new van first had to winch it off, then winch the old one on, manoeuvre to the new position, winch it off, pick the new one back up again and drop it off in the space that the old one originally occupied. To complicate matters, Baby Face indicated the wrong position for the old van to be moved to, so the new van was placed in the way, and the old one had to be winched straight back off, then the new van winched back on, moved out of the way, then finally winched off again. That sounds quite complicated, and the delivery driver certainly thought so, because after the fifth manoeuvre, he lost his rag and called Baby Face something very rude.

I don't know why people say moving house is one of the most stressful things you can do because, despite the messing around with the delivery man, we managed to do it in less than half an hour. And the beauty of Baby Face's new home was that everything was in there, ready to go. And I mean *everything*. Because it was a show home, all the beds were made up, there was shampoo and a rubber duck in the bathroom, a bowl of plastic fruit on the table, a plastic chicken in the oven and several family photos in brass frames on the mantelpiece (not his family of course, but seeing as he'd fallen out with his real one, he decided to keep them).

He'd made sure the two vans lined up, so that the back door of his and the back door of mine were more or less face to face, with only a small gap between them. We got a friend of a friend who worked for Jeckells Sails of Wroxham to make us a small strip of canvas that sealed the gap between the door frames, then took my door off its hinges, so that only Baby Face's remained, acting as an interconnecting door between the two vans. This meant that I'd be able to visit him and he'd be able to visit me, without us having to brave the elements in winter. We agreed that we wouldn't cross the threshold without invitation – after all, it wasn't like we were going to be living together – and we fitted some knockers and doorbells on either side of the door, which we got as a two-for-one deal at the Trading Post DIY shop, which was having a closing down sale. We also went into Blyth & Wright to get two engraved brass plates to go outside our main doors, so that visitors would know whose van was whose. His plate said 'Archbishop's Cloisters' and mine said 'Copeman Palace'. While we were there, I also got some little badges to go on the doors to the various rooms in my palace. The kitchen-diner was christened the Drawing Room, the main bedroom was the Royal Suite, and the bathroom was the 'Throne Room'. There was a small second bedroom in the Palace, which I didn't have any plans for at the time, so I didn't bother getting a badge, seeing as they cost £3.99 each.

After Mumsy had helped me give the van a good spring clean and put some rather fancy burgundy-coloured velour throws over the seats, Baby Face came round to the bungalow in his car to help me move my stuff. I remember my first night in the Palace, closing the interconnecting door behind me, then heading into the Royal Suite and snuggling up in my sleeping bag. Up until now, being a king and having an empire had just been another hobby to help keep the tedium at bay. I suppose it still was, but it somehow seemed a little more real now I had my own palace.

At Buckingham Palace, Queen Elizabeth would probably be finishing off her Horlicks and tucking herself in for the night too. I thought to myself that maybe we weren't all that different really, apart from our age and gender of course. As I let off a silent, beef-flavoured Pot Noodle fart, I felt at peace for the first time in a long time.

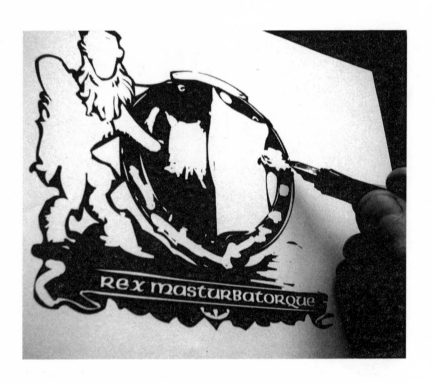

7

Empire Building

A great empire and little minds go ill together.
EDMUND BURKE (1729–1797)

We quickly got into a routine at the Palace and Cloisters. The highlight of the week was Saturday night, when we held the 'Chinese Lottery' in the Cloisters. Despite Baby Face's new-found wealth and our mutual success at swindling the Housing Benefit Scheme, the night was still an extravagant expense for gentlemen of our humble means and did, on occasions, cause some serious cash flow problems.

I'd ring the doorbell for the interconnecting door at around sixish, and we'd don our wizards' costumes, fill our goblets with Irn-Bru and have a game of chess. At ten past eight we'd start to feel a bit peckish, so we'd switch on the TV and tune in to the *National Lottery*. It's not that watching the lottery in itself stopped us being hungry, it's just that we'd developed a system whereby the numbers chose what we'd be eating for dinner.

Because Baby Face and I are always arguing over things, such as what channel we should watch or whose turn it is to put a quid in the electricity meter, we have learned that the easiest way to solve most disputes is to toss a coin, or take it in turns to have casting votes. But when it comes to dinner on a Saturday, we let Dale Winton's balls do the work.

Our local Chinese takeaway is the Lotus House, of 10 Station Approach, Sheringham. Their menu is a bit weird in layout, but effectively breaks down into two sections: the main dishes, numbered 1–129 and the 'B' dishes, numbered B1–B79. (There are also some 'S' dishes, denoting 'specially very hot spicy dishes' – as HP always says, the proprietor seems to like adjectives almost as much as monosodium glutamate) and combination meals A to F and BA to BC. But for the purposes of the Chinese Lottery, we ignore the hot dishes and combination meals (they're for show-offs and unimaginative people respectively).

When the first ball comes out on the lottery, we order the corresponding main dish number. When the second ball comes out, we add 40 to the number, then order the corresponding dish, again from the main section. When the third ball comes out, we add 80 to its number and do the same again. That way, each dish from the main section has an equal chance of getting selected (except for dishes 41–49 and 81–89, which overlap into two ranges of balls – this is a problem we have yet to sort out).

The fourth ball selects the 'B' dish. So the available range is B1–B49, not right the way through to B79, which, as it turns out, is perfect, because it misses off the expensive duck dishes (which at £29.50 for a whole duck and 24 pancakes could bankrupt us) and the mingy squid dishes that appear in the B70s.

The fifth ball determines which two-litre bottle of pop we take out of the fridge to go with our meal. 1–16 is Cherry Coke, 17–33 is Orange Fanta and 34–49 is Sprite. If it's Cherry Coke, there's always a dispute, because Baby Face likes his at room temperature, whereas I – like any normal person – like it chilled.

The sixth ball selects which pudding we get out of the freezer. 1–16 is Wall's Vienetta, 17–33 is Co-op Strawberry Cheesecake and 34–49 is Sarah Lee Fruits of the Forest Gateau.

Finally, the bonus ball selects which after-dinner chocolates we have. We always have at least three boxes in stock, bought from Nobby's for a pound a box. 1–16 is Teacher's dark liqueur chocolates (my favourites), 17–33 is Cream Liqueur milk chocolates (Baby Face's favourites) and 34-49 is Cointreau dark chocolates (which we both hate as much as each other, but the risk of getting them adds to the excitement of it all).

So on Saturday, 25 October, we had:

No. 4: Chicken and Noodle Soup
No. 10: King Prawn with Green Peas
No. 18: Sausages, Peas and Chips
No. 21: Chicken, with Pickled Ginger & Pineapple
No. 43: 2-litre bottle of Sprite
No. 49: Sarah Lee Fruits of the Forest Gateau
Bonus Ball, No. 15: Teacher's Liqueur Chocolates

This came to £18.30 in total, which is £9.15 each. A king's ransom by anyone's standards, especially mine. The main reason that meal sticks in my mind, in particular, was because Baby Face had declared in advance that that evening we'd be holding a summit, and that he would be taking minutes of what happened.

Baby Face is forever declaring one thing or another with immense gravitas, when in fact it's usually something totally irrelevant. He once typed up a six-page document detailing the 'Gingersnap Clause of 1999'. I'd just made a cup of tea and had run out of biscuits. He had one gingersnap left and refused to let me have it. He knew I always have to dunk at least one biscuit in my tea because I'm highly superstitious about things like that. He also knew, like I did, that by the time I'd got to the late-night garage and back, my tea would be cold and it would be too late, and I'd probably be cursed for ever. So he agreed to give me his last gingersnap, on the condition that I would allow him a once-in-a-lifetime casting vote on any matter we might be disputing in the future.

According to the document he typed up, there was a strict procedure for executing the clause, which would be set in motion upon his issuing of the command, 'I hereby invoke the Gingersnap Clause of 1999'. I would then be duty-bound to concede on whatever issue was being debated, even if it was a matter of life and death. We'd both signed the document at the bottom of the last page, witnessed by Roy Boy and some trucker who just happened to be at the truckstop having his breakfast bap at the time.

Now, as I tucked into the gateau, Baby Face started scribbling away in his notebook and going on about what a landmark moment the coronation ceremony had been and how, with the creation of Copeman Palace and Archbishop's Cloisters, the Empire now had a real, physical presence – a stronghold, from which to launch its bid for world domination. It was strange listening to Baby Face talking about the Copeman Empire like this – it was just something I'd made up after all, but he was talking about it like it was a real entity that had real ambitions. He can under no circumstances be described as charismatic, but this is the one occasion I can remember when he came close. I could see the passion and determination in his eyes. Maybe this was something worth being king of, after all, and I decided to play along.

Baby Face reckoned we'd need something to rally around, like a flag or a national anthem – maybe both. Every great nation had them, along with a load of other mugubbins. I told him I was a little concerned that this whole thing could turn silly if we weren't careful. I mean I was up for an impressive-looking coat of arms, maybe a catchy national anthem to rouse the spirits on a damp morning when we were riding over to the Job Centre, but I didn't want to be doing anything tasteless. Baby Face assured me it'd be class through and through. Looking at his purple-jeans-and-red-hunting-jacket combo, I wasn't convinced that he would be the best judge.

As we munched away on our Teacher's liqueur chocolates and polished off the last of the Sprite, Baby Face noted down all the stuff the Empire would need, to look as established and powerful as it was fast becoming. A fly on the wall would have thought we were two big-time diplomats planning something important. And, in a sense, we were.

Because I was skint at the time, I decided to get most of the stuff done in black and white, with the simplest design, to save money. Most flags are gay affairs, but the one I designed looked slightly sinister – it was just split in half, vertically, with black on one half and white on the other. The Commander is always tutt-tutting when he sees a Union Flag (apparently it's only a 'Jack' if it's on a ship) being flown the wrong way round. I can never understand how you tell if it's the wrong way round – it looks exactly the same to me both ways. But so that I, too, could be snobby about my flag, I decided to have a little white patch in the bottom corner of the black bit – the flag is supposed to be flown with the patch at the bottom, mast-side.

Baby Face's mum and dad like to do things with style. They have two concrete lions outside their house, have sprayed their wheelie bins silver and write all their letters on cream water-marked notepaper that has an impressive-looking crest on it that says 'Stride Forth' underneath. As King, I'd have to maintain simi-lar standards, so one Sunday, when the Commander was round for lunch, I asked him to help me ink up a coat of arms with a black and white shield and Gothic 'CE' initials (for 'Copeman Empire') in the middle. He's very arty and even has a calligraphy set. I wanted an impressive motto underneath, and he suggested we use some Latin, because apparently all the best mottos are in Latin. He selected the chunkiest nib from his calligraphy set and carefully wrote 'Rex Masturbatorque' underneath the crest, which I thought looked a bit rude, but he assured me it was some kind of sombre oath dating back to the reign of King John.

Mumsy's very good on the sewing machine, but unfortu-nately there are some fiddly jobs she can't do too easily these days because she got carpal tunnel syndrome a few years back. So I went round to see Beryl Patterson, who does all the costumes for the local Gilbert & Sullivan Society, to see if she could make a medieval-style coat for Noel Edmonds, with Gothic patterns all over it and a hood thing to go over its head, like the sort of thing I'd seen at a medieval war recreation day in Holt a few years back.

But it turned out that the material was going to cost a fortune, and she said she was too busy making spandex catsuits for a local heavy metal band to take on such a large project. Then I had the idea of making a scaled-down version that'd fit Honey, which would cost less in material and be a lot quicker for her to make. When I told HP, he thought it was a ridiculous idea, but Mumsy thought it was brilliant, and I phoned Beryl to arrange a time to take Honey round for a fitting. In fact, Beryl came round to the bungalow because she didn't want to get dog hair in her house. Honey didn't like wearing her new suit at first and kept trying to scratch the hood off, so Beryl ended up having to cut it off, which was a bit of a shame.

I decided I could do with some royally themed clothes of my own, mainly for wearing around the Palace, because I remained a bit self-conscious about going out wearing fancy dress. When the Commander is relaxing in private in his flat in Norwich, he likes to wear what he calls his 'romper suit', which is a sort of two-piece tracksuit with a hood, made with that distinctive towelling material they use for babies' all-in-one swaddling suits. He looks quite a sight with his hood drawn up tight around his face, with just his spectacles and beard poking out, sipping a pink gin. So I got Beryl to make me my own romper suit, with a few royal embellishments, inspired by a picture I'd come across in a magazine of Prince Charles wearing a dashing ceremonial uniform at St James's Palace. Beryl said uniforms tended to be made out of slightly cardboard-like woollen material, but we opted for some nice navy fleece instead, which would be far more stretchy and comfortable for lounging about in at the Palace.

I was so pleased with my romper suit when it was finished that I got Baby Face to take a photo of me wearing it, relaxing on the sofa, watching *Trisha*. I thought Prince Charles might be interested in getting one himself, so I sent a copy of the photo over to him, care of St James's Palace, telling him how great it was and drawing attention to some of the features, such as the concealed remote control pocket and the Velcro flap on the seat, to help make visits to the throne more convenient. I enclosed Beryl's contact details and suggested he get in touch with her next time he was in Norfolk visiting Sandringham.

When I was out and about, I'd usually just dress in jeans and a jumper, a bit like Prince William when he went off to St Andrew's University. After all, I was a king, whether I dressed in full uniform or not. The only indication that I had royal connections was a small metal crown badge that I picked up in the 50p box at the Kit Stop in East Runton and wore pinned to my chest.

For smarter mufti occasions, my suit from Mr Green was perfect, though the only tie I had was a Simpsons one that Mumsy got for me one Christmas. I'd noticed that Prince Charles and Prince Philip were often to be seen wearing stripy club ties, but the only club I'd ever been a member of was the Youth Club, and most boys that went there were far more interested in getting a go on the table tennis or squeezing Rachel Hyams's tits than getting matching ties and reclining in leather chairs with pipes and copies of the *Telegraph*. If the Empire were to have a club tie, I decided it'd have to be something in black and white so it'd go with the flag. Using the Internet at the library, I came across an Austrian-based discount tie store, which sold all sorts of high-quality stripy woven silk ties, one of which was black and silver. Baby Face and I both bought one, and wore them when we were out on official state business.

Now I had my own fixed address and a fancy royal crest, I decided it was time to get myself some letterhead paper. HP had a contact at Rounce & Wortley Printers who could do me engraved letterheading at a really good price. He says that you can tell a lot about someone from their stationery, and he always insisted on using engraved paper and cards when he was doing business, even though it cost a lot more than standard printing.

In fact, the man at the printers suggested I go for 'thermographically raised type', which looks just like engraved type but is cheaper to produce and is safe to run through a laser jet printer. I handed over the Commander's ink crest, selected the type of paper I wanted and approved the typeface, and a week later a big box of five hundred 120gm woven white sheets were delivered to the Palace, along with three small boxes containing the business cards. They looked absolutely exquisite: the crest and motto at the top – which looked very sharp scaled down – and 'Copeman Empire' printed underneath, in capitals, in an elegant Garamond typeface. At the bottom, in small black type, was my address at the caravan park. One rub of a thumb over the raised lettering, and you instantly knew you were dealing with someone of real class.

When you live in a small town, your every move and word is scrutinised – one small slip-up and everyone soon knows about it. Now that increasingly important national business was being discussed, I felt we had to do something to protect state secrets. As the Commander says, 'Careless talk costs lives.' I once remember overhearing a prayer group – not a Salvation Army one I might add – where a group of ladies were huddled together over tea and wholemeal biscuits, supposedly praying for people, though in fact using it as a way of passing about the latest gossip. One of the ladies started off, 'Dear Lord, we pray for Rachel Hyams, who's caught a sexually transmitted disease from either Darren Chambers, Kevin

Cape, Jeremy Venables or Toby Carr' ... then she opened one eye and looked round to check that everyone was suitably astonished by these revelations, and continued, 'We pray for her in her time of need, may the rash and discharges quickly go away, in Jesus' name, Amen.' Everyone said Amen, raised their eyebrows and tut-tutted, then it was someone else's turn to say a 'prayer'. With prayers like these, you need to be careful what you get up to.

I remembered back to when I was at school and people used to put on funny voices to hide what they were saying during lessons. Nick Cook and Grant Williams always used to go around calling people rude things in strange choir voices, so it was almost impossible for the untrained ear – i.e. a teacher's – to work out what they were saying. A rather more sophisticated technique, which I have since learned wasn't exclusive to our school, was Egg Language. The theory is simple. You just say 'egg' before every vowel in a word. So if you'd forgotten your gym kit, and Mr Swain wanted you to do it in your underpants, you could say to his face, 'Meggistegger Sweggain eggis egga teggossegger', without getting into trouble. Baby Face got rumbled in the Lower Fifth though, when a new, twenty-something teacher called Mr Morgan joined the school. He remembered Egg Language from when he was a boy, and didn't take too kindly to Baby Face calling him 'Sheggeep Sheggaggegger Meggorgeggan'. He went bright red and told him, 'Theggat's deggeteggenteggion feggor yeggou, yeggou leggittlegge sheggit.'

Still, Egg Language became very useful as the official language of the Copeman Empire, allowing Baby Face and me to talk openly between ourselves in public, under the pretence that we were learning Swahili – something that Mumsy proudly told her friends at the Sally Army coffee morning.

One of the members of what likes to consider itself the local in-crowd is Pete Fowls, who's a bit of a toff and lives in Blakeney. He and his brothers all wear signet rings on their little fingers, with some posey family crest on it, which I always thought looked rather impressive. I made enquiries at the local jeweller's, but could no way afford to get my own signet ring made with the Copeman Empire crest on it. So in the end, I came up with the idea of boring out the middle of a one-pound coin, to make a ring that – though inexpensive – looked pretty classy from a distance. HP helped me drill the hole out in his shed, and then smooth it up with a conical-shaped sander attached to his drill. It fitted very nicely onto the smallest-but-one finger of my right hand. Written around the edge is *'Nemo me impune lacessit'*, which the Commander told me is Latin and means, 'No one harms me without punishment.' I thought that was rather cool, like no one was going to mess with the King, or something. But Fowlsy scoffed at it, saying it probably meant no one harms the coin without punishment, in which case I was going to be in trouble.

Baby Face, who has always been very musical and can do a touching rendition of 'Yesterday' on the kazoo, wrote a Copeman Empire national anthem, sung to the tune of 'Thine be the Glory,' usually after an Irn-Bru too many:

Fine Copeman Empire,
Ruler of the Sea,
Under Fearless Nich'las
Shepherd of the free.

Out through perilous waters
To the Copeman Isle,

Guiding us victorious
With his boundless guile.

Fine Copeman Empire
Ruler of the Sea
Envy of all nations
Ever home to me.

8

World Wide Empire

As the Empire must extend,
So let extend thy mind o'er all the world.
JOHN MILTON (1608 –1674)

To say that I have no friends would be totally inaccurate. I have *loads* of mates, such as Baby Face of course. And Andrew Waters. Although Andrew is 18 stone, has a slightly odd-sounding voice and works for BT installing fibre-optic cables, he's actually a good bloke.

North Norfolk recently got broadband, so he's been very busy for the last few months hooking new customers up to the Information Superhighway. Apparently a lot of old people have insisted on signing up, even though they don't have a computer. They don't know what they're missing. Every time I log on, I am struck by how cool it is. After all, if it weren't for the Internet, I'd never have discovered UK Deed Poll Online and become a king.

As I say, I like Andrew, even though he can be a bit annoying and self-important at times. He lives on his own above Dave's 2* fishbar, which is where he gets his breakfast, lunch and dinner. Andrew insists that his weight problem is due to his being big-boned, compounded by an unusually slow metabolism and a rare glandular condition. Baby Face once told him, 'You're a fat bastard because you eat shit and don't exercise.' Andrew and Baby Face don't get on.

When Andrew isn't laying cables for BT, or eating chips in Dave's 2, he's in his flat, surfing the Net. He's obsessed with the SAS, MI6 and JFK, and always tries to get people to call him by the nickname he's given himself, which is '@', pronounced 'at'. He claims he needs to use it to hide his identity, but no one can be bothered. He can come out with some pretty ridiculous stories actually, and is always insinuating that he has connections with the British Intelligence Service and that fibre-optic cable laying is merely a front for clandestine communications activity on behalf of GCHQ. I told him that he doesn't look much like James Bond, but he said that neither did David Shaylor. Andrew says he'd never blab about what he gets up to – you'd have to feed him his own testicles before he cracked. Andrew doesn't seem to have any friends to speak of, except me, so whenever I'm about in town and he sees me from his window, he'll shout down and ask me up for tea and chips.

---

*In case you're wondering, Dave No Surname owns two fish bars in Sheringham – 'Dave's on Cooperative Street, and the imaginatively entitled 'Dave's 2' on the High Street, next to Hunt's and opposite the clock tower.

One Sunday afternoon, I popped round to Darren's newsagent for some Transform-a-Snacks. As I was coming out, Andrew shouted down to me, so I went up to see him. He wanted to show off his new computer, which he told me was 'the dog's bollocks', because it had twin Pentium 4 3.6 Ghz processors, with 1024Mb of RAM. It had this space-age-looking display system, with three flat-screen monitors arranged in an arc, which looked rather out of place in his scruffy bedsit. He wasn't doing much in particular, just playing around with a computer program that lets you build websites. He wasn't actually designing anything, so I asked him how hard it'd be to make a website for me. I'd even buy him some chips to say thank you. He said, 'No problemo, baby' (I forgot to mention, he has a slightly strange way of talking, too), and that if I threw in a two-litre bottle of cherry cola he'd do it for free, even though his BT standard callout rate was £50 an hour.

In just a few hours, we'd got the basics of a site together, all themed around me being a king and having an empire – not dissimilar to the British Royal Family website in fact, which we kind of ripped off. Andrew thought that if we could add some good photos, it might even fool slightly gullible people, Americans perhaps, who would maybe think I really did run an empire, which they could visit on holiday.

As Andrew quite rightly said, 'You gotta sell the sizzle, not the steak,' so we hammered everything up, being economical with the truth and generous with my grander vision of what the Copeman Empire could be. We stuck in a timeline that went back to the 1700s, showing that the Copeman Empire had quite a heritage, but was just so secret that very few people ever knew about it. A bit like that film *Forrest Gump*, where he kept turning up at critical moments in history, playing a pivotal part, but going

unnoticed. Andrew helped register www.kingnicholas.com
for me and, £39.99 and twenty-four hours later, the site was up
and running.

Baby Face popped in once or twice to see what we were up
to, but he and Andrew kept arguing about stuff that had nothing
to do with the website, like whether Snickers was a better name
for a chocolate bar than Marathon. Baby Face prefers Marathon,
and still insists on asking for it by its old name in Darren's. But
Andrew argued that 'We work in international markets and
product branding needs to be rationalised across territories to
provide a coherent merchandising policy.' He also said that, as
Marathon became Snickers almost ten years ago, along with
Opal Fruits becoming Starburst, there really was no point debat-
ing the matter.

Andrew told me about this thing on the Web, which was all
the rage, called 'Blogger', which lets 'idiots' publish their own
online diary. I decided to become a royal blogger, posting my
regal musings on the site, to update what I hoped would be
increasing numbers of subjects on what was happening with the
Empire. Both Uncle P and the Commander told me they'd
checked it out when they were in Norwich Library.

After a month of the site being up and running, Andrew said
he'd been checking the site stats to see how many people
had visited, and all sorts of other details such as where they were
from, which pages they'd looked at and how long they'd looked
at them for. He'd printed out some pages with lots of tables and
pretty pie charts. When I looked at the number at the top of the
sheet, I almost fainted. The total number of hits for Week Two
was one thousand six hundred and fifty-two.

1,652

Just seeing that number again makes me feel queasy. I couldn't believe it. My school had just under 1,000 people in it, and I can still remember what an impressive sight it was when we were all lined up on the tarmac playground for the fire drill at the beginning of every term. The Headmaster had to stand on the fire escape steps of the sports hall and use a megaphone to address us. Even then we couldn't hear him. And that was only a thousand people. Twice that (if you round up to the nearest thousand) had visited my empire online. Twice as many people as there were at my school had, metaphorically speaking, lined up on the tarmac of the Copeman Empire and I had stood on the fire escape and spoken to them through a megaphone.

Andrew said that, in fact, 1,652 referred to the number of 'hits', which, for reasons I didn't understand, didn't mean they were all people looking at the site. He told me that 'visits' were a more accurate measure of how many people had been to the site, and I'd scored 856. He said this in a very sniffy way because apparently that's a pretty crap amount of traffic in the grand scheme of things.

But 856 was, to me, still a bloody good score. About as many people as stood on the concrete playing area for the fire drill at school, minus the staff. And for someone who'd never had anyone really want to listen to him, except for Baby Face, and occasionally Andrew, the idea that 856 people could, in just one week, come along and want to find out more about me and my empire, just blew me away.

Andrew's stats broke down visitors by region, and they were coming from everywhere: America, Canada, France, Germany, even 16 people from Korea, 5 from Iraq, 3 from Libya and 1 from Jersey. For someone like me, who had rarely travelled further south than Ipswich, the idea that I could set up an empire that would reach people on the other side of the world, all from a bedsit above a chip shop, was totally amazing.

N·R ROYAL MAIL POSTAGE PAID GB BIRMINGHAM MC5

Miss Zara Anne Elizabeth Philips
c/o Gatcombe Park
Minchinhampton
Stroud
Gloucestershire
GL6 9AT

On His Majesty's Service

9
Prince Charming

It felt amazing. I don't know how I did it
and I don't know if I will be able to repeat it.
ZARA PHILLIPS (1981–FOREVER)

f you ask me, girls are fascinating creatures – a bit like boys, but more temperamental and nicer smelling. For some reason, I've never been all that successful with women. I think the girls round Sheringham must just sense that I'm far more sophisticated than the other boys and reckon I'd be well out of their league. I wouldn't be, of course – it's just the impression I like to give, as part of my mating ritual.

Now I was a king, I was hoping I'd stand a better chance of pulling some A-grade totty, like the blonde lifeguard at the Splash Leisure Centre, who I'm sure I caught eyeing me up while I was paddling about in the shallow end one morning. In fact, I think the only reason I've taken a liking to her is because she looks quite a bit like my true love – the girl I one day hope to marry.

Zara Phillips.

The dream now is always the same. One day, my phone will ring and it'll be Princess Anne saying, 'Hello Your Majesty, Princess Anne here. Don't know if you can help, but I'm looking for a suitable husband for my daughter Zara. She's ended up with a right rough-looking brute who's covered in bruises and smells like a men's changing room. It really is a nuisance. I'd like her to marry into a good family and we all know there's only one royal family held in more esteem than the Windsors, and that's the Copemans. She really is very nice, don't let that ghastly tongue stud of hers put you off.'

I am still waiting for that call, but when it comes I shall be straight down to Westminster Abbey to tie the knot. All the British Royal Family will be there, of course, and I might take a moment to counsel Prince William on the challenges that lie ahead of him as King, seeing as we're both about the same age, and I've pipped him to the post.

Even before I became King, I often wrote to Zara. Though she hasn't said it herself, I feel I am quite possibly her 'rock', just like Paul Burrell used to be Diana's. Except I'm not camp and am certainly not one to gossip, unless the information is particularly juicy. Nor have I ever been accused of making off with my dead employer's belongings, but that's mainly because I've never been employed, let alone by someone who's dead.

I regret that some of my letters haven't quite struck the tone I'd like. I am always after a kind of Prince Charming effect, but I think that sometimes I can sound a tiny bit desperate, which is certainly not my intention. One of my best letters to Zara was actually written with a lot of help from Baby Face. It was made all the more impressive by using a computer-generated, hand-writing-style typeface called 'Bradley Hand', which Andrew had on his computer and which offers all the sophistication and elegance of genuine handwriting, coupled with the convenience and efficiency of word-processing. More love letters should be written by computer if you ask me.

I actually hope that Zara doesn't like the letter too much, seeing as Baby Face wrote it, because it could all turn out like that film where an ugly girl writes love letters on her attractive, though less articulate, friend's behalf. But when the bloke who receives the letters finds out they weren't actually written by the attractive girl, he decides to dump her and go out with the ugly, articulate one, because he's really connected with her and believes love is much more about two minds coming together than anything else.

Seeing Zara and Baby Face together would be too much for me to take.

Copeman Palace

Beeston Regis Caravan Park

Sheringham,

North Norfolk NR25 5GH

Miss Zara Anne Elizabeth Phillips

c/o Gatcombe Park

Minchinhampton

Stroud

Gloucestershire GL6 9AT

Dear Zara,

It has been almost a week since I last wrote to you and, already, I feel I must write again. My emotions are running at such a pace, I am having trouble keeping up with them in my mind, let alone keeping you informed by letter. I am looking forward to some kind of reply, which you haven't yet made, probably owing to your equestrian sporting commitments.

I think my previous few letters, especially the one I sent to your mother telling her what a 'hot catch' I'd be for you, may have struck the wrong tone. After all, I am not some kind of oddball sending crazed letters – though I am sure you can tell that by the classy letter headed paper I am using (in case you're wondering, it's 'thermographically-raised' type, rather than 'engraved', which the printers told me is a more cost-effective way of achieving a very similar effect – it also allows me to run it through the printer – yes, believe it or not, this is actually typed, not written). Of course, a fruit-case would not go to such lengths – in fact, I believe they tend to cut out letters from a newspaper and stick them onto blank paper, using rubber gloves, so they don't leave any fingerprints.

Though I still have raw passion for you aplenty (as evidenced by the enclosed photograph), I feel I must also prove to you that we could have a long-term relationship, soundly based on common interests and a similar back-ground. So I have also sent a copy of this letter to your father, who can look it over and advise on my suitability.

And it seems our families have crossed paths before ... my father tells me he worked alongside your grandfather at Wall's Meat Company in the Sixties – your grandfather as a senior executive, and my father as a promising manage-ment trainee on the sausage extrusion line. My father later left meat and moved into the maize-based snack industry, just as it was about to explode (not literally!) and has quite a stash as a result, both of crisps, which he still gets sent to sample even though he's retired, and a three-figure number of shares in KP Snacks, which means that I'm pretty well set up for the future, and wouldn't dream of sponging off you in any way.

In a further effort to harmonise my lifestyle with yours (and let's face it, we have a lot in common already) I have altered my style slightly. I read in Heat Magazine about celebrity couples often looking like one another, so I popped into Scissorhands Gentlemen's Barbers of Sheringham with a picture of you on Saturday, and got Chris Marshall – the senior coiffeur – to cut my hair short, just like yours. (I always did like your hair when it was shorter, and hope you will return to that look once we get together.) I have an interview with the Royal Navy soon, and needed to get my hair cut to regulation length, and thought it a coincidence that I could have hair like yours and fulfil the requirements of the Admiralty Interview Board. Of course, both your father and your stepfather were Captains in the Navy. And surprise, surprise, my family has a strong naval tradition too – my father was a Midshipman on National Service and my uncle was a Commander in the Supply & Secretariat, until he was invalided out because of his knees.

By the way, do you still have a tongue stud? I had toyed with the idea of getting one myself, if only to say that I have shared your pain, but I'd rather not go through with the procedure, especially if you no longer have it – apparently they can be a bit of a health risk.

I have been getting a lot of riding practice lately and

am actually starting to do it quite well, occasionally breaking into a slight trot on the way back from the Job Centre.
My confidence has grown such that I no longer have to ride
side-saddle and I am now thinking of taking up polo. On
the subject of Polos, I can do a very clever trick where I join
two of them together like cable links, but with no obvious
join. I would include an example, but fear it might get
crushed in the post, or make the letter heavier, therefore
requiring another stamp.

I must draw to a close now, because I want to keep you
hungry for more and, if I shrink the typeface slightly from
11pt to 10pt, I should be able to fit this letter onto one piece
of paper, which, at 84 pence a sheet, is rather expensive, even
for letters expressing deepest sentiments to a lover.

With all my love, vigour and respect (I am talking to
you, Zara, not your father, who will also be reading this –
as I say, I have sent him a copy, though on cheaper paper,
and sent second class).

Nicholas
HM King Nicholas

10

The Royal Bank of Copeman

Greed ... is good.
GORDON GEKKO (1941–)

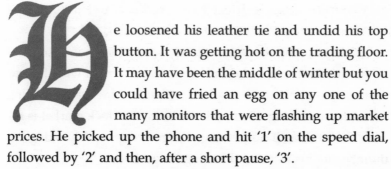e loosened his leather tie and undid his top button. It was getting hot on the trading floor. It may have been the middle of winter but you could have fried an egg on any one of the many monitors that were flashing up market prices. He picked up the phone and hit '1' on the speed dial, followed by '2' and then, after a short pause, '3'.

'Look, I ain't got time for chit-chat. Put me 40 on WPP now ... yeah, the Five Eights Account.' He waited a second for confirmation, then slammed the phone down. There was a hiss as he flicked the lever on his leather seat and reclined, looking down his nose at the computer screens as the numbers danced, hypnotically, like neon fireflies. He took a sip on his double espresso. It had gone cold in all the excitement, but it'd be two hours yet before he could duck out for more.

The morning had started out well, until, for no apparent reason, his shares in IPM Construction had taken a downturn. In a panic he'd offloaded them all, but it was only a temporary dip and the price soon went back up – beyond the opening price – without him, and he'd lost out heavily as a result. He was hoping to make it up now, on WPP. After all, Sir Martin Sorrell, the biggest doomsayer in the industry, had just made positive predictions for End-of-Year, and he might be able to make a few quid on the back of the good news.

The screens refreshed. WPP was up. He breathed a sigh of relief. Maybe he could recover his position after all. His shirt was wet with perspiration and he was starting to feel the chill as his adrenaline levels subsided. He glanced at the monitors once more, before swivelling his chair round to face his protégé.

'You see, Nick. This ain't no game for pussies. Even a bad-ass trader like yours truly can have a bad day. You just gotta roll with the punches and hold out for the money shot.'

I had to admit Andrew certainly seemed to be in command of the situation, even if I didn't understand a lot of what he was saying, due to the odd lingo and slightly American-sounding accent he was using. 'Betting is for boys; the stock market is for men,' he said, as if addressing a large group, and hooking his thumbs into his belt and thrusting his groin out.

He walked over to his Panasonic plasma TV and stuck a DVD on, skipping through it with the remote and picking out bits of interest. He told me it was called *Wall Street* and that it was the 'dog's bollocks'. He showed me a few clips of a bloke called Gordon Gekko, one of the most feared Wall Street traders of the Eighties, who I thought looked a bit like Michael Douglas. Andrew told me that Gekko made millions with his hardball business tactics and 'you wouldn't see him wasting time on the National Lottery – the odds just don't stack up'. Andrew obviously loved Gordon Gekko, because he couldn't stop grinning as he watched him.

Then he showed me some screens on his computer, and told me, in a nutshell, how he used the HSBC website and his telephone to trade on the markets, buying and selling shares in publicly quoted companies. He said the odds were much better than conventional betting and, even if you were a novice (not that he was, of course), you could make a killing. He said that recently he'd been doing so well he'd even thought about going part-time at BT, so he could spend more time on his 'trading floor', which doubled as a sitting room. I tried to play it cool, as I imagine any of the City boys who Andrew told me about would, but I just couldn't hide my excitement. There was something about all those screens, flashing up numbers and information, that meant you couldn't just watch and do nothing. The more I watched Andrew in action – buying, selling and drinking his little cup of strong coffee – the more I wanted to roll my sleeves up and get stuck in myself.

It took me a while to get my head round how it all worked. Andrew talked me through all the different figures and graphs he had at his disposal on his computer and, as he was showing me all this, he ran a copy of *Wall Street* off onto VHS to take back to the Palace with me 'to help me get into the groove'. Andrew was so impressed with Gordon Gekko that, as well as having a big poster of him on the wall above all his computer screens, he'd even sampled clips of his voice off the film and somehow loaded them into his Roland keyboard, so he could press the keys to make slightly disjointed sentences. When he got it just right, it sounded like Gordon Gekko was actually in the room talking to you.

Over the next few weeks, Andrew took me under his wing, and I think he rather enjoyed having someone to mentor. He even started calling me 'Buddy', after Gordon Gekko's own protégé in the film. He gave me all the benefit of his experience and tips from his contacts in the City. Andrew said he doesn't get down to the City very often because he's not supposed to use his BT van for personal trips, but he proudly showed me his photo album of past visits to various meetings in London, with him standing alongside people in suits, who he told me were big players in the top FTSE 100 companies, in which he had shares. He said he only had one or two shares in each company, but that didn't stop him receiving the annual report or going down to the Big Smoke to meet the top brass face to face at the annual general meeting, and grilling them for information.

His pride and joy was a photo of him with some bloke called Sir Martin Sorrell, who I hadn't heard of before, but is, apparently, some big shot in the media world, even though he only came up to Andrew's armpit. Andrew had had the print blown up to A2-size at Snappy Snaps and hung it on the wall above his George Foreman Grill. He told me that Sir Martin's business, WPP, which originally stood for Wire and Plastic Products, was once a near-worthless PLC that made shopping baskets, but that he'd bought it for peanuts and turned into one of the biggest media groups in the world.

I asked whether I could have a go at trading myself, on Andrew's machine, but he said it was far too powerful for my abilities and instead set me up on one of his old PCs, which he said was pretty fast, by early Nineties standards. Later on, he accompanied me over the road to HSBC and helped me fill out a load of forms for a business account, which, it turned out, I'd be eligible for, even though I was unemployed. He suggested I set up separate trading accounts for my different activities so it wouldn't get confusing when the markets were busy, because even top traders are prone to making errors. He told me he'd named his two main accounts '88888' and 'Teldar', the first being the same number as the account that Nick Leeson used to bring down Baring's Bank, and the second being the same name as the company whose AGM Gordon Gekko attended, in order to make his infamous 'Greed is good' speech.

I decided to call my accounts 'Copeman Empire' and 'Universal Exports' – the first for obvious reasons and the second as a tribute to the company name that James Bond uses as a cover story when he's on a mission.

My HSBC business card arrived a few days later and I was very impressed. It said 'HM King Nicholas' on it in embossed letters, and the enclosed letter told me that as soon as I'd signed it, it was ready to go. Andrew handed me a special pen he said he used for writing on the surface of his compact discs and I signed the shiny strip on the back of my new card with a flourish. I couldn't wait to try it out, so I immediately went over the road to Darren's, to make my first ever purchase on plastic. It was a real buzz as Darren ran my card through the machine and it gave a chirpy 'beep', before a slip of printed paper came out of the machine, which he asked me to check and sign.

When Darren saw the name on the card, he shook his head and said, 'Well, I never', before handing it back to me, along with my receipt and almost £20 worth of sweets, pop and magazines, which I took back over the road with me, to share with Andrew.

Unfortunately, Andrew only had one phone in his flat, which he used a headset to operate, so if I wanted to place any orders I had to run over the road to HSBC, which became more of a problem as I became a better trader, because if there was some old lady in front cashing a giro I could get held up, often missing out on the faster market moves. I decided that as soon as I could afford one, I'd get myself a mobile.

Andrew thrived on the risks involved in trading and said he'd become addicted to living on the edge, like most of the traders in London and New York. Andrew is allergic to peanuts, but told me that on slow trading days, he'd sometimes play Russian roulette with a bag of Revels*, just to satisfy his addiction to adrenaline.

I was never all that good at maths when I was at school, but I seemed to have a natural feel for how the markets moved, and Andrew was more than happy to take care of the 'back office' tasks relating to each trade I made. I didn't have too much money to speculate with, but one day, when I was round at the flat, Andrew got in a big flap about something he spotted on one of his screens and shouted at me to 'Go big on EMI'. I placed everything I had – just over fifty quid – on it. It was tense stuff, because almost the moment we put our money on, the value started falling. My pulse was racing – that

---

*Revels have since replaced the peanuts with raisins, and Andrew has been forced to seek his thrills elsewhere.

money had to last me the week and I hadn't even bought the groceries yet – but then, at around midday, the value suddenly lurched upwards on the back of some good results and, at four o'clock, I followed Andrew's lead and sold out for £148.63 after bank charges.

I felt light-headed with excitement. Andrew was really pleased with how I'd kept my nerve. He even bought chips for our dinner that night. They were the best chips I'd ever tasted.

The next day, I went into Hunt's. I hadn't been in before, because it's very exclusive and would normally have been well outside my price range. But not now I was a successful trader. He had a nice blue shirt in my size, with a white collar and cuffs, which looked quite similar to the sort of thing Gordon Gekko wore. Mr Hunt seemed a bit suspicious when I offered to pay with my credit card, especially when he saw the name on it, but after popping out the back of the shop for a few minutes he came back and everything seemed to be in order. He ran my card through the machine and, again, there was a bleep as it was accepted, followed by a chug-chugging noise as the receipt was printed out, ready for me to sign with my flourishing royal signature. I decided I could get used to this.

As I strolled down New Road, swinging my designer shopping bag by my side, I decided to pop into Scissorhands to get a new haircut. I asked Chris to give me a slicked-back look, like Gordon Gekko. Chris knew all about Gordon Gekko – in fact he was a bit of a fan himself – so he knew exactly what I was after and splodged a big load of Brylcreem on at the end. I bought a tub of the stuff off him, to take home with me to the Palace.

Next day, I had a look in the window of the mobile phone shop and made enquiries about getting a Pay As You Go handset. I didn't want to rush into making a decision though, and decided to hold off, at least until I'd had a chance to ask Andrew for his advice, seeing as he works in the telecommunications industry himself.

11

Impolite Society

Rather a tough customer in argeyment, Fowlsy,
if anybody was to try and tackle him. [Copeman]
CHARLES DICKENS (1812–1870)

I don't know what the exact benchmark for success is. But I suppose having a new BMW 3 Series with M3 alloys, a semi-detached house on the 'right side' of Blakeney and a girlfriend who looks like Michaela Strachan off *The Really Wild Show* is a pretty good start. Which is why Pete Fowls, who has all of these things and a whole load of other stuff, including a chrome fruit-juicing machine and smoothie blender, makes no secret of the fact that he considers himself to be one of life's successes.

Fowlsy used to go to school with me and Baby Face and was very good at rugby, whereas Baby Face and I were more into our badminton. Nowadays, most of his rugby mates are more into drinking than playing, and they all have team shirts with the letters of the alphabet on the back to show who can down a pint the quickest – something they're always keen to contest down at the Crown Inn. ('A' is the fastest and 'Z' is the slowest. Fowlsy tends to hover around the 'D' mark, which equates to about six seconds.)

He can, at times, be a bit full of himself, and sometimes takes the piss out of me a bit more than I'd like, but he's certainly worth keeping on the right side of, not least because he's so generous when it comes to buying drinks. (Most people in Sheringham keep a mental bar tab for everyone they know, and I was recently reminded by Matthew Curtis that I owed him a pint of Adnams, dating back to the one he claimed he got me on New Year's Eve 1994.)

One night, Fowlsy and I were sitting in the snug bar of the Two Lifeboats Hotel, killing a bit of time before we had to go off to our respective social engagements – he was meeting his girl-friend for dinner at Marmalades Bistro and I was going to be heading back to the Palace to watch *Derren Brown: Mind Control*, over ham and pineapple pizza, with Baby Face. Fowlsy had got the drinks in, and I'd asked for a pink gin, just to keep the naval training up.

We were sitting in one of the alcove windows discussing London fashion, which Fowlsy's really in to, when I spotted Andrew walking past outside. He immediately caught my eye, gave me the thumbs-up and headed for the front door of the pub. I knew there could be a problem. Andrew and Fowlsy dislike each other almost as much as Andrew and Baby Face do.

Andrew came into the bar with a big grin on his face but, upon seeing Fowlsy, suddenly frowned, and Fowlsy muttered something under his breath. Andrew came over, said hello to me, then sat down, placing an Evian bottle, which he'd refilled with Ribena, on the table.

I tried my best to get the conversation flowing, asking Fowlsy whether he'd had his new hands-free kit wired into his BMW by the garage yet. But before Fowlsy could answer, Andrew butted in and said wired-in hands-free kits were 'so yesterday's technology' and that Bluetooth was the way forward. He told Fowlsy he should get a Sony Ericsson P910i as well, if he could afford it. Fowlsy took some offence at this and said of course he could afford it, he was the Marketing Manager of Fowls Concrete, for God's sake. Andrew sneered at this and said the only reason Fowlsy was the Marketing Manager was because it was his dad's business. This made Fowlsy even more angry and he maintained that business acumen ran in his family's genes and that he was appointed Marketing Manager at a young age through talent, rather than through family favouritism. Andrew just rolled his eyes and said, 'Yeah, yeah, you keep telling yourself that, sunshine.'

The situation was deteriorating rapidly and it became clear by the looks I was getting that both Fowlsy and Andrew were expecting me to back them up. I was starting to feel very uncomfortable – both of them were my mates, and I was caught in the middle.

I suppose Andrew is just a bit jealous of Fowlsy's lifestyle and the fact that he has loads of fancy gadgets, like a PDA, a laptop and a girlfriend, none of which Fowlsy really knows how to use, and which Andrew says are a waste of good technology. As for Fowlsy, I think he's just like a lot of people who mistake Andrew's brusque manner for someone who's arrogant, rather than someone who's just very intelligent and also a very interesting bloke once you get to know him.

Fowlsy started getting quite abusive to Andrew, rudely referring to his weight, and telling him he was a loser and that his job at BT was crap. He downed his pint and said, 'Come on, Nick, let's leave fatso to drink his Vimto. How about a drink at the Lobster? I doubt Walters will fit through the door.'

As much as Fowlsy was a mate, I thought that was well below the belt and, as I pointed out, Andrew was actually drinking Ribena, not Vimto – you could tell by the colour. I enjoy a bit of banter and mickey-taking as much as the next man, but I was stunned when Fowlsy suddenly turned on me and said that if I wanted to stick up for 'Mr Blobby', then that was just fine – 'You deserve one another.'

I tried to calm the situation down – after all, if Fowlsy were happy to apologise for being rude to me and Andrew, then I would be happy to let the matter lie. But Fowlsy wouldn't listen and, in one last rant, accused my empire of being a sham, said that everyone around town thought I was a tosser and that, if I fancied myself as some kind of celebrity, I was about as big-time as Jonathan Wilkes. I asked who Jonathan Wilkes was, and he said, 'Exactly', and left, leaving me sat at the table with Andrew and with everyone in the bar staring at us. I was seething, but Andrew was as cool as ever, and took a slurp on his Ribena, before suggesting that we head round to his flat to watch *Hollyoaks* instead.

12

Meet and Greet

Then, welcome each rebuff
That turns earth's smoothness rough,
Each sting that bids nor sit nor stand but go!
Be our joys three-parts pain!
Strive, and hold cheap the strain;
Learn, nor account the pang; dare, never grudge the throe!
ROBERT BROWNING (1812–1889)

I was pretty pleased with how things were going with my empire. I had an impressive title, smart new clothes, was renting my own home, and developing the makings of quite a career in the world of finance. But not everyone seemed to be sharing my enthusiasm. Baby Face said he'd heard on the grapevine that Fowlsy had been in the Lobster, slagging me off to anyone who'd listen.

I was really shocked. I'd known Fowlsy since I was eleven and, while we'd always been far too different from one other to be best mates, and often used to fall out and then make up again, I'd thought we always had a genuine respect for one another. Obviously not.

I suppose it would just take some getting used to, for people to understand that I was no longer just plain old Nick Copeman, and that I suddenly had a bit of get up and go, and wanted to make something of myself.

Baby Face said Jesus had the same problem, because he suddenly claimed to be the King of the Jews, but all the locals already knew him well and just said, 'No, you're not – you're Joseph the Carpenter's son.'

Becoming King might have started off as a joke, but I was starting to get quite attached to the idea. Even though it was pure invention, the change seemed to give me extra confidence to go and do stuff, as if I had a reputation to live up to. I wondered what I'd need to do to convince others that I was fit to be a king.

Baby Face reckoned the problem was that I was getting too caught up in the nuts and bolts, when I really needed to be step-ping back so I could see the bigger picture. He said no one was going to care about me and my empire if I stayed indoors all day and no one ever got to hear about it. And while he could see that my King Nicholas website had some merit in it, along with all the trading activity, I really needed to get out there and meet more people – generally spread the word. He said that was why the Queen went out looking at hospitals and schools all the time, instead of staying at home watching TV, or fiddling around with the Royal Family website – she needed to be out there pressing the flesh and maintaining a strong presence. Although Baby Face isn't a real man of the cloth, there was something very thought-provoking about his counsel. It was almost like a Damascus moment, and I couldn't sit still for the rest of *Emmerdale*. Baby Face was right. It was time to spread the word.

I was really geed up and wanted to do something straight away. Baby Face was always complaining that I wasn't impulsive enough, but tonight would be different. Tonight, the King would take the lead, and his Archbishop would see what he was really made of.

I went into the Royal Suite and got changed into my suit and I told Baby Face to put something smart on too, which, in his case, was his red hunting jacket and a pair of corduroy trousers. We both put our Copeman Empire ties on, checking they were straight in the Throne Room mirror.

I hadn't even decided where we were going and what we were going to do, but if Baby Face reckoned we should get out there and meet people, then that was exactly what we'd do. I rummaged through the cupboards above the settee in the Drawing Room until I found what I was looking for – a box of black and white flags that I'd bought when we first started getting all the Copeman Empire memorabilia together. Andrew had found them for me online, at some kind of nautical whole-salers. Andrew knows Morse code, semaphore and all sorts of other communications lingo and had told me that at sea the signal flag for '6' was black and white. He got a brilliant deal for buying bulk, and I decided to get 100 instead of 50, as it wouldn't cost much more for the extra. As it turned out, we never found a proper use for them, and Baby Face had started using them as hand towels.

I still wasn't sure what I was going to do with them, but I stashed a few handfuls in a Morrison's bag and handed it to

Baby Face to carry. I was dog-sitting Honey for a few nights because Mumsy and HP had gone down to London to visit Clare, so I decided Honey could come with us in her medieval coat, so she'd get a walk at the same time as we took care of state business.

It was dark outside, so Baby Face brought his Maglite, and we walked over the recreation ground towards Nelson Road. I'd decided that we'd just speak to whoever we bumped into – whether we knew them or not – and tell them a bit about ourselves and the Copeman Empire, just to raise awareness. We'd got as far as the council estate on Lawson Way and still not met anyone, so Baby Face suggested we try knocking on a few doors. I wasn't so sure and thought we'd be invading people's personal space, but Baby Face accused me of being a Kentucky Fried Chicken, so I had no choice. The adrenaline was pumping as I walked up to the first house on the corner – Number 44 – and rang the bell. In fact, I almost bottled it and ran off, but Baby Face was blocking the way, and I turned back to see that the door had been opened and a man in his fifties was standing there.

When I'd dreamt up this half-baked idea of meeting people, I'd visualised myself being really charismatic and greeting everyone I met with a firm handshake and looking them straight in the eye as I introduced myself, as King Nicholas, before proceeding to tell them all about my wonderful new empire.

In reality, I ended up giving this bloke a limp handshake and mumbling some inane nonsense about how I lived on the caravan park and was just out visiting people. He couldn't understand what it was I wanted exactly – I didn't really know myself – and we were left standing there, both unsure what on earth we were doing. Baby Face broke the silence by offering him a flag, which only served to make the bloke even more confused. Still, after a little persuasion from Baby Face, he agreed to take it and we said goodbye.

I felt really stupid, but Baby Face was very impressed and thought I'd deliberately stood there saying nothing, just to spook the guy out. After meeting just one person, I'd had enough, and wanted to go home. It was a totally pointless idea coming out in the first place. But Baby Face insisted we visit a few more houses. After all, the first house was bound to be the hardest, and I'd soon get into the swing of it.

It was very strange meeting people we didn't know and who didn't know us, without any real reason whatsoever. But after a few houses, my awkwardness seemed to wear off a bit and I managed a pleasant smile as people answered their doors. It was fascinating how people seemed to draw their own conclusions about what we might be wanting, without us prompting them in any way. And having Honey with us turned out to be a good idea too, because she's very pretty, and most people couldn't help but give her a pat and some even gave her treats.

A few people said they'd already heard about me and asked what all the fuss was about. I didn't have any grand mission statement, so I just said something vague, about how it was all about personal empowerment. I didn't know what that meant exactly, it was just something I'd heard Andrew going on about once, round at his flat. Baby Face was much better at meeting and greeting than me. I'm forever surprised, and perhaps a little jealous, at how uninhibited he is when dealing with people. He was only too happy to intervene when my conversation dried up, and tell people all about his Zinger Faith and how it had changed his life.

We just expected to have a quick chat on people's doorsteps and certainly hadn't planned on entering anybody's home, so it was a real shock when we got our first invite, before I'd even managed to say a word to the person who'd answered the door.

I'd knocked on a door – number 26, I think it was – and a man in his forties, wearing a sweater, trackie bottoms and a pair of maroon slippers with gold lions on, answered and said, 'You took your time.'

I hesitated for a moment, but he ushered us into his sitting room and asked us if we'd like tea, which I turned down but Baby Face accepted – white with three sugars – and we stood by the radiator, wondering what to do, while he popped next door.

Baby Face was as confused as I was and I whispered to him that we should leave. But he insisted we stay and see what happened – this was the warmest welcome we'd had so far, after all.

The bloke came back with Baby Face's tea and seemed a bit surprised that we were just standing there doing nothing. He looked down at Honey then looked back up at us. He could obviously tell that something wasn't right.

Then he asked us where our tools were.

Baby Face busked it and said they were in the van. The man went over to the window, pulled back the net curtains and peered outside, then said, 'What van?'

He was highly suspicious by now, and came straight out and asked us, 'You are here to fix the TV, aren't you?'

When I explained that I was a king rather than a TV repair man, he seemed very confused, even though I thought the explanation was simple enough. I gestured to Baby Face that we should get going, pronto. But Baby Face insisted on finishing his cup of tea, and I had to endure several more uncomfortable minutes, with the bloke wondering what exactly we were doing in his living room, and me wondering exactly the same thing.

Baby Face said afterwards that he knew exactly what he was doing – he was having a cup of tea.

Not everyone welcomed us with open arms – I suppose door-to-door work attracts undesirables as well as kings doing their rounds – and we got quite a few firm rebuttals, the odd aggressive dog and one person who refused to come to the door, despite the fact that we could see signs of life inside, and Baby Face rang the doorbell and banged on the window several times. If someone was out, I'd take out a business card and jot down a quick note on the back with my fountain pen, saying the King had called round with his Archbishop and we were sorry to have missed them. This was quite expensive, at fifty pence a card.

What was strangest about the whole door-to-door thing was that so many people assumed we wanted money when, in fact, we'd just popped round for nothing in particular and made no requests for cash whatsoever. On several occasions, people's first words to us would be 'who are you collecting for?' and at one house a lady didn't even ask that, just ducked into the other room and came back with her purse and offered us a pound.

I wasn't quite sure what to do, but Baby Face said that, seeing as there was no real reason to our visits, it'd probably just be polite to accept any donations people wanted to give us without making too much of a fuss. It wasn't like we were doing anything dishonest – we had overheads, after all.

We called it a day just before ten, because we wanted to get back to the Cloisters in time for *Yes Minister*, and figured most of the people we were visiting would probably want to do the same – as Baby Face said, it is a classic, after all. Back at the Cloisters, sipping on a mug of Mint Chocolate Options, I was finding it hard to concentrate on the TV. I was really excited by how well we'd done – meeting and greeting. I'd felt so awkward to begin with, but after a while, I'd really got into the swing of it and my self-confidence had grown a tremendous amount as a result. Andrew is always going on about the team-building weekends he goes away on with BT, and I reckon Baby Face and I had achieved a similar effect, and without having to go off hiking in Wales.

Everyone on Lawson Way now knew a bit more about King Nicholas and the Copeman Empire and would be able to put people straight if they heard them gossiping about me. And we'd picked up £13.26 in the process, without even really trying. I wondered, what would happen if we tried a bit harder?

13

Charity Work

Charity begins at home.
SIR THOMAS BROWNE (1605–1682)

here's a nice lady who lives at the end of Mumsy and HP's road, called Cherry Blois-Brook. She's very active on the charity circuit and is often to be seen with a collection tub and a load of stickers in her hand, campaigning for one thing or another. She's always looking for helpers and had managed to press-gang HP into collecting for the Norfolk and Norwich Association for the Blind.

He spent a morning standing outside Moss Pharmacy, taking donations from local shoppers and, a few days afterwards, he received a note from Mr K.M. Hodson, one of the fundraising organisers, thanking him for his help and saying that the charity had raised a total of £492.80 that day, of which £41.93 had been raised by HP.

I was amazed that HP could make so much money in a

morning and asked him what his sales technique was. He said he didn't have a sales technique as such, in fact you weren't even allowed to rattle your tin these days, because it had been banned by the local by-laws. He said you just had to stand there and wait for people to put money in of their own accord, then offer them a little sticker off the roll. He said the odd person would ask what he was collecting for, and one person asked him if he was blind himself, to which he answered 'no', but other than that, he didn't have to do much really, except stand there and look friendly.

I was having a chat with Baby Face about this, and he really liked the idea of collecting money. He said that nowadays, as there was little demand for royalty to lead armies into battle, most of them tended to get involved in charity work of one sort or another, and setting up community projects such as the Prince's Trust or the Duke of Edinburgh Award scheme. In fact, he reckoned I should set up a charity of my own.

Over dinner, which was a very tasty recipe of mine (leeks, with a melted Dairylea and crushed bacon crisp topping), we formulated a plan.

Baby Face said that when he'd been visiting Norwich recently, he'd got caught in a pincer movement by two excitable young charity workers in Day-Glo bibs, one of whom started break-dancing in front of him to catch his attention, while the other – a vivacious blonde – swooped in from behind and almost knocked his chicken burger out of his hand. Apparently, she then started rattling off a load of facts about starving children in Africa, with a big smile on her face. Baby Face said that this was a new breed of charity workers, who were paid professionals, and he said they seemed to take their work very seriously and he later saw them all having a group huddle on the corner of St

Stephen's Street, as he was making his way back towards the station.

I told him it sounded far too energetic for my liking and we'd be better off just standing there and seeing how we got on, like HP had done, rather than wearing ourselves out by running around and waving our arms about.

Still, I agreed with Baby Face that we should approach the whole exercise professionally and pay ourselves an hourly rate – me as Chief Executive and him as marketing director – along with a performance-related bonus. Baby Face assured me that any remuneration would pay for itself at the end of the day, what with the added motivation factor.

We couldn't decide exactly what we'd be collecting for, but thought we could work that out later, depending on which causes seemed worthy enough at the time. For now, we'd just be content to go out and collect money, then deposit the proceeds, minus any overheads, in a new charitable trust that I'd set up at the bank.

I thought a good name for the charity would be 'The King's Trust', which Baby Face liked too, and we made a list of all the things we'd need to look the part – such as a collection tub, promotional stickers and ID cards.

I remembered that I once had a red plastic collection tub, back when I was in the Cub Scouts and did a Bob-a-Job Week, shining people's shoes in the foyer of HP's old office. Later that night, I popped round to the bungalow and had a root around in the loft. I eventually found the tub in one of the boxes of my stuff, along with some A-Ha and Bangles cassettes, which I took back with me to the Palace to listen to, for old times' sake.

Because I bite my nails, Baby Face had the task of scratching all the Bob-a-Job labels off the collection tub while we watched *Newsnight*. The next day, I popped round to see Andrew at his flat during his lunch break, to see if he could print me up some labels and a couple of ID cards. He was a bit reluctant because he said he'd had quite a bit of work on lately, what with BT offering free broadband connections. He was also doing a fair bit of trading at night too – on the Japanese markets – so all in all, he was pretty flaked. Still, once I explained exactly what we needed the stuff for and how much we were hoping to collect, his ears pricked up and he said he might be able to find a little time to help me out. After all, it was for charity, and he didn't mind doing his bit for charity, as long as he wasn't left out of pocket.

Andrew pointed out that charities don't get their promotional materials for free, and even the likes of Amnesty International have to pay their marketing people. So if he were going to be making promotional materials for me, then he'd expect to be paid a little something for his time.

I didn't like the idea of incurring too many costs before we'd even started collecting, so I came to an agreement where I didn't have to pay Andrew anything up-front, just 20 per cent of the takings, to cover the cost of his labels and time.

Andrew had to rush off back to work, but he agreed to meet up with me again later that evening, when we designed a 'King's Trust' label to go on the collection tub, a photo ID card for me and Baby Face, and lots of little stickers, which we could give to our donors.

By Thursday morning, Baby Face and I had finalised our plans and got all the kit ready. He was impatient to get out there as soon as possible, but I reckoned we should hold off until Saturday, when it'd be nice and busy in town, hopefully with a healthy sprinkling of wealthy visitors up from London for the weekend, with plenty of disposable income that we could help them dispose of, straight into our collection tub.

On Saturday, at ten a.m., Baby Face and I walked into town and took up our positions outside Moss Pharmacy. I was holding the collection tub and he was holding the stickers. We'd only been there a few seconds, and were still acclimatising, when we were taken by surprise by our first punter – a man in brown slacks and a green quilted jacket who was walking in the direction of Bertram Watts and stuck what looked like a fifty-pence piece into the tub as he walked past, giving us a smile as he did so. Baby Face didn't even get a chance to offer him a sticker, because he didn't slow down to give us his money. He just carried on down Church Street, before turning into the Co-op.

Baby Face and I looked at each other, gobsmacked. As Baby Face said, the man couldn't even have known what we were collecting for, and for all he knew it could have been for 'Blind Dogs for the Blind'. He was just lucky that we were a respectable king and archbishop, out collecting for a worthy cause.

I'd barely had time to ponder this before our next benefactor appeared – a little boy in a duffel coat, accompanied by his mother, who stretched up to put a one-pound coin in the tub. I had to bend down a bit, so he could reach. Baby Face peeled a King's Trust sticker off the sheet and stuck it on his coat, and did the same for his mum. Then off they toddled, up Station Road.

Baby Face started whistling the Copeman Empire national anthem. This was going to be a piece of cake – and a rather nice chocolate one from the Craft Bakery, if we kept receiving donations at this speed.

There was a bit of a wait for our next donor – an elderly lady with a tartan shopping trolley who I noticed checking us out as she went into the pharmacy, and who then came up to us on her way out. She seemed pretty sharp for her age and looked us both in the eye and said good morning, before leaning towards me to squint at my tub. She seemed perfectly happy, and nodded and said, 'Ah, the King's Trust – good, good', before reaching into her coat pocket and taking out her purse, and producing two five-pence pieces, which she popped through the slot, one after the other. I couldn't help thinking of that story in the Bible, where the old lady puts her last two coppers in the collection tin. I wondered whether she wouldn't be a pretty strong cause for charity herself – she certainly looked very thin, and in need of a good Zinger Tower Meal. I thought I could feel a slight pang of guilt, but dismissed it as mid-morning tummy rumbling.

A few people we knew bumped into us and said hello, and were a bit surprised to see us collecting for charity. Frank Chandler, who lives on the same road as Mumsy and HP and has known me since I was a baby, was very suspicious and started asking all sorts of awkward questions about what the King's Trust was and what it raised money for. He seemed quite unconvinced by my explanation, which was a bit feeble and something to do with it being a trust fund for the disadvantaged. I held up my ID badge to reassure him, but he didn't seem impressed.

Unfortunately, it started to rain quite hard, and Baby Face said we'd have to use some of the collection funds to buy an umbrella. He darted over to Darren's, who must have seen the change in the weather and quickly swapped the price tags, because Baby Face ended up paying £9.99 for a flimsy green brolly that had a smiley frog's face printed on it and nylon legs sewn on at the front, which flapped about in the wind.

Luckily, I was wearing my Chris Bonnington mountaineering jacket, so I just pulled up the storm hood and drew my left hand up inside its sleeve, leaving the right one out to brave the elements and hold the tub.

Despite the rain, we had an equally steady stream of donors – some more inquisitive than others – but mostly happy to do their bit for charity and hand over some money to the Copeman Empire's new charitable trust. The highlight came when a bloke in a puffa jacket, out with his girlfriend, stopped when he saw us, took out a wad of cash held together with a bulldog clip and pulled off a tenner. He folded it up to put it in the slot but, unfortunately, it wouldn't fit. So Baby Face – rather too hastily for a bona fide charity worker, I felt – snatched it off him and put it in his pocket, before decorating his puffa jacket with not one, but two King's Trust stickers, presumably to mark him out as being an extra-generous donor.

Baby Face mentioned that charity workers usually get their lunch provided free, courtesy of the organisation they're collecting for and, seeing as we'd had such a good morning's collecting – despite the bad weather – he suggested we give it another ten minutes, then take a lunch break.

There were only three and a half minutes to go when I suddenly sensed that not all was quite right. I'd become aware of a tall man in a dark overcoat, standing over by the clock tower, watching us. People often stand around in Sheringham watching the world go by, so it wasn't all that strange in itself, just that I sensed he was taking rather too much interest in us, specifically. We'd just taken another donation, from a woman who said she'd 'give a pound to anything as long as it's not for animals', when I saw him look both ways and cross the road, heading in our direction. I just had time to say, 'Uh oh', under my breath to Baby Face, before he was upon us.

'Morning gentlemen', he said, in a voice that sounded distinctly police officerish.

The game was up. I looked down at my feet and mumbled a 'hello'. Then he asked what we were collecting for, addressing me, seeing as I was the one holding the tub. I was momentarily tongue-tied but, luckily, Baby Face intervened and answered on my behalf.

'We're collecting for the King's Trust.'

The man then asked what the King's Trust was, and Baby Face gave his little speech, which he'd perfected during the course of the morning, about how the trust had been formed to help disadvantaged members of society, who were particularly vulnerable during the winter months.

The man didn't say anything. I knew we'd had it. I just kept staring at the floor.

But then I heard the distinctive sound of a coin hitting the bottom of my collection tub – a two-pound coin by the sound of it – and I looked up to see that he'd dropped some money in. I couldn't believe it. I looked him in the eye for the first time and, without smiling, he said, 'Keep up the good work, lads – it's good to see young people taking an interest in others.'

And with that he left, walking off down the High Street in the direction of Matella. My jacket might have been made out of breathable 2-ply Gore-Tex, but I suddenly noticed that I was damp with sweat. Baby Face was a bit spooked out too, and we decided to call it a day and quit while we were ahead.

We went into Dave's 2 and ordered two All-Day Mega Breakfasts, to celebrate our success, then sat down to count our spoils – stacking the coins on top of the ten-pound note from the bloke in the bomber jacket.

Baby Face did some sums – totting up our various receipts and expenses, and deducting them from the cash on the table. We'd done brilliantly well and collected a whopping £49.65. But, after our various operating expenses had been deducted – a frog brolly, two cans of cherry cola, two bags of Space Raiders, a packet of Werther's Originals, some spare batteries for Baby Face's Walkman, two All-Day Mega Breakfasts and, of course, our hourly wages and five per cent performance-related bonuses – we were left with just £14.58.

We were a bit disheartened and Baby Face said he wondered how much money given to other charities ever got to the people it was really meant to help, when so much of it seemed to get absorbed by unavoidable administrative costs.

After our lunch, I popped upstairs to see Andrew and give him his twenty per cent cut, which I'd worked out to be £2.92. But he insisted that his cut was to be taken out of *gross* takings, not *net*, which, according to the calculator on his PDA, was £9.93. There seemed to be no negotiating with him so, reluctantly, I took a load of coins out my pocket and started counting out his money.

He said he didn't want a load of 'shrapnel', and snatched the scrunched up a ten-pound note out of my hand. He was quite reluctant to give me the seven pence change too and said he couldn't understand what all the fuss was about – he could earn way more than we did in a whole morning, just by activating a broadband connection, which only took him half an hour to do.

I went over the road to HSBC to deposit the remaining £4.65 into the new King's Trust account I'd set up, thinking how pathetic it seemed. Not that Baby Face and I had decided what we were going to do with the proceeds, but I'd at least hoped

we'd have enough to do something nice like send a disadvantaged family off to Pleasurewood Hills for the day.

That night, back at the Palace, Baby Face and I were having a chat about the day's events. Baby Face said it was important not to get too disheartened. Even if it turned out we'd only done a little for charity, that was better than doing nothing at all, and, at the very least, being seen out and about looking busy would all help boost the profile of the Empire. He suggested that – rather than giving up at the first hurdle like so many well-wishers seem to do – we should keep going, making our collections a weekly event and perhaps visiting a different town or village each week, so we could do our bit for charity and get to have a nice day out, exploring new places, at the same time.

I really liked the idea and reckoned that with a bit of fine-tuning to our technique, and with a few less overheads next time round, we might do a lot better. I suggested that, before our next trip, we should bodge a hole in the top of the collection tub, so that next time, people would be able to roll up their banknotes and pop them in more easily.

That night, as I sat watching *The Bill*, I had a sense of well-being. I'd never really understood the concept of charity before – as Baby Face always used to say, 'What's in it for me?' But now I understood that you could get almost as much out of giving as you could out of receiving.

14

Duchy Unoriginals

So man did eat angels' food.

THE BOOK OF COMMON PRAYER

HP had bumped into Frank Chandler at the Splash Leisure Centre, who'd mentioned that he'd seen me out collecting for some strange charity that he'd never heard of. HP knew nothing about it, but guessed that it was probably another of my scams and, when I was round at the bungalow later that morning with Baby Face, watching *Zena*, he started interrogating me about what I'd been up to. I don't think my explanation was very convincing and he got in quite a strop, saying that if he found out I'd been doing something dishonest, I'd be in big trouble. Baby Face felt a bit uncomfortable and said he was just popping to the loo, but then didn't come back.

I realised I'd have to start humouring HP if I were to keep him on-side, and I already had the early makings of a new venture, which I thought he might approve of.

An empire marches on its stomach, and I had my eye on snacks.

Success in the snack business has come naturally to my family. As well as HP, my cousin Terry (he's Mumsy's nephew) works at Kettle Chips in Norwich, as Production Manager. Which means he gets loads of free crisps. Which means I really like him, because he's always bringing freebies round when he comes to visit.

He sometimes brings new flavours that are still in development for us to sample. They always come in plain foil bags and he has to be quite secretive about exactly what's in them, because, as he keeps telling us, the premium snack food market is a highly secretive and competitive world.

He can't carry too many bags at once though, because he rides a motorbike – one of those hardcore Japanese racing ones – and he doesn't have a saddle box, because he says it upsets the aerodynamics, and if he were going to upset the aerodynamics, he'd have a pretty girl on the back instead. His motorbike is very noisy, and Honey always barks at him when he arrives on it. Terry says it's noisy because it's got a racing spec exhaust pipe, which isn't strictly for road use, but he's peeled off the label that says 'Not for road use', so no one will know.

If I'm honest, I've always been a bit jealous of Terry, not least because he's had a string of beautiful girlfriends over the years. He recently got himself a new one, who didn't like riding on the back of his motorbike and made him buy a second-hand sports car with his end-of-year bonus, so he could take her out without her getting her hair all messed up.

One weekend, Terry came round to show us his new car and his new girlfriend, who he introduced as Porsche. I thought Porsche was his girlfriend's name, a bit like one of those women on *Footballers' Wives*, but then I realised that it was his car that was called Porsche and that his girlfriend – who he introduced only after showing us Porsche's leather interior and sports gear shift – was called Katy. HP was most impressed, both with Porsche and with Katy, and turned to me and said, 'You could be a success like Terry, if you were a little more intelligent and worked in the food industry.'

HP and Terry always have plenty to chat about, what with HP being the snack industry equivalent of a Vietnam veteran, and Terry running the production line of one of the region's most respected, up-and-coming premium snack food businesses.

While HP and Terry obviously know a lot about making crisps, I like to consider myself a leading authority on the consumer end of the process, and probably eat more crisps than the two of them put together, which is quite an achievement, seeing as Terry gets as many as he wants free, and HP is rarely to be seen without a bag of something or other in his hand.

I have long been on a quest to find the ultimate snack. I am still searching. Once in a while, though, something close to snack nirvana comes along, and I feel privileged to have experienced, with my own lips, some of the pivotal moments in snack history, when a product comes along that taps into the aspirations of a generation – the crispy equivalent of the Beatles in the Sixties or Noel Edmonds in the early Nineties.

For example, Spicy Flavour Transform-a-Snacks, circa 1993, were in my opinion the closest that low-cost maize-based extrusions have come to perfection. Pringles came close to reaching the mid-priced, reformed-potato snack holy grail, but while I agree that the shape is one of the marvels of modern scientific design, the flavourings have never been sophisticated enough to appeal to my palate. Kettle Chips have certainly got the crispiness but (and I'd never say this in front of cousin Terry, of course) a lot of the flavours just seem a bit too 'in-yer-face'.

And of course, no discussion of the history of snacks could pass without due homage being paid to Phileas Fogg, which almost single-handedly pioneered the premium snacks sector, and galvanised HP's position as the godfather of adult nibbles.

Baby Face has always been a bit of a philistine when it comes to savoury snacks. He's into his pork scratchings and little else, and every time he opens a bag, he comes out with the same crap joke, about how they're just like Rachel Hyams: 'Rather tasty, but not the sort of thing you'd want your mum to catch you eating.'

For me, the benchmark for a good crisp is just the conventional, ready-salted variety, without any fancy shapes or weird flavours – just pure, unadulterated, potato crisp. I'd discovered, quite recently in fact, that one of the best examples of the plain crisp is the 'game chip', which I first tasted at the Rat Catchers when all the family went for a pheasant lunch to celebrate Mumsy's birthday. I didn't really like the pheasant, even though it had a nice sauce on it that tasted a bit like Irn-Bru, and I hurt one of my teeth on something hard in the meat, which I later found out was a piece of shot. Still, the game chips were brilliant, and when I asked Mumsy who made them, she said, 'The Chef', which I assumed must be some obscure snack brand from France that I hadn't heard of, until HP pointed out that she meant 'the chef', as in the bloke in the kitchen who cooked the food. Mumsy said that anyone could make game chips in fact, and that she had a recipe for them in one of her cookbooks at home.

I was absolutely amazed that there was a recipe for actual

crisps and that you could make them yourself, without a big factory and the specialist skills of someone like Terry or HP. I'd always assumed that snack-making was left to the experts, like dentistry. But no – according to Mumsy, anyone could have a go. I asked Mumsy to show me the recipe as soon as we got home, but she put her foot down, saying she wouldn't have me making crisps in her kitchen, because she'd just had new Corian work-tops put in and she didn't want fat splattered about all over the place. She'd been going on and on to HP about how great Corian is and how she just had to have a new kitchen made out of it, even though HP said he thought it was a right rip-off. It looks just like marble, but, according to Mumsy, and the brochure, it doesn't get corroded by lemon, is highly heat-resistant, scratch-proof and has no visible joins. Mumsy even paid extra to have a burgundy-coloured stripe run right around the edge, just to be extra flash. I'm not a Corian salesman, incidentally, though I can genuinely attest to the fact that it doesn't get corroded by lemon, is highly heat-resistant, scratch-proof and has no visible joins, even when looking for them with a magnifying glass. But Corian is not for me. I have plastic-coated MDF in my caravan, which I'm very happy with. It might take a few knocks and scalds, but in my opinion that all adds to the character.

I told Mumsy that if she wouldn't let me make crisps in her new Corian kitchen, then I'd just have to make them round at the Palace. Mumsy was very worried at the idea of me boiling up hot fat in a confined space, especially as I didn't have a fire blan-ket any more, since Baby Face had used it as a bath mat. But Mumsy knows all about my obsession with crisps, which goes right back to when I was a kid and I first started sticking peanuts inside barbecue Hula Hoops to make little vol-au-vents. She knew that now I'd got hold of the holy grail – a recipe for crisps

– I wouldn't let it rest until I'd made some, even if it meant second-degree burns. So to stop me getting hot fat all over myself – or even worse, her Corian worktops – she suggested she buy me a deep-fat fryer, so I could run an extension cable out into the garden and make them out there, where she could keep an eye on me. I had a look in the Argos catalogue and picked out the cheapest one they had, a Breville DF9C with two-litre oil capacity, long-life, anti-odour charcoal filter and removable safety locking lid – all for just £19.95. Next time I was over in Cromer, at the Suntan Centre, I popped in on the way back to buy one. But, unfortunately, they'd sold out, and the only other one they had in stock – from the Antony Worrall Thompson Professional Series – cost a whopping £69.99, which was well outside Mumsy's budget.

I was really disappointed, but when I saw HP back at the bungalow, he was rather sniffy about the idea of my getting a deep-fat fryer, and said they were only popular with the under-belly of society, and a rather large underbelly at that, given the sort of disgusting, unhealthy things they tended to cook up in them. HP had been feeling rather smug lately, because he'd cut right back on all his snacks, gone on the Scarsdale Diet and started doing light workouts at the gym three times a week, losing over a stone as a result. This meant he now fitted into a lot of his favourite suits from the early Eighties, which brought back good memories because that was around the time he got his big promotion at work and received all sorts of perks, including a bigger office and his first Volvo estate.

But when I told him I wanted a fryer so I could produce crisps, he suddenly got all excited. I think it was because I used the word 'produce' rather than 'make'. 'Make' is what amateurs do, 'produce' is what professionals do. He must have thought I was going to be following in his footsteps, getting into full-scale snack food manufacture. He told me, for the umpteenth time, the story about how he first met the founders of Phileas Fogg, running their business out of a Portakabin at the back of the British Steel depot in Consett, how he went in, looked over the business plan, gave it the thumbs-up and the rest was maize-based snack food history.

He took me into his little study, cleared a pile of newspapers off his old armchair and offered me a seat, under the shelf where he keeps his plastic business awards, standing next to a minia-ture plaster bust of Socrates. The last time I'd sat in his study was when I failed to get into university, and we had a man-to-man chat about what I should be doing next, over a glass of sherry, which he keeps in the top drawer of his filing cabinet along with a multi-pack of McCoys crisps and all of his bank statements.

I told him my basic plan was to make some kind of butter-fried game chips, using sweet potatoes, because I thought they'd be tasty, and he started nodding his head and making a sort of purring noise, which he often makes when he's eating, or about to eat, some crisps. I remembered that when I was little, Mumsy had bought a weird contraption called a 'mandolin' at a good homes show, which lets you slice and dice vegetables, and make all sorts of other funny shapes with them. At the time, HP said she'd been ripped off and that it was just a cheap gimmick. She was adamant that it was a good buy because it came with three extra attach-ments absolutely free, along with a complimentary set of premium kitchen knives whose handles, unfortunately, ended up falling off the first time they went through the dishwasher. After a few weeks of having all sorts of oddly shaped vegetables with our meat chops, she cut her thumb quite badly on the thing and chucked it (the mandolin) into the back of one of the cupboards.

There it had remained for almost ten years until now, when out it came again, for the wafer-thin slicing of my new crisps.

I can't say too much about the production of my 'King Nicholas Butter Chips', except that they're longitudinally cut, wafer-sliced, semi-caramelised, butter-fried, sweet potato chips, made the traditional way, in a heavy-duty metal coal bucket slung over a fire. Any more information than that and you'd have to be an authorised King Nicholas Butter Chips Production Director, fully signed up to the company non-disclosure agreement. HP and I toyed with the idea of letting Terry try our new super-chips. But HP reminded me that snack-making could be as cloak and dagger as the IRA, and you only had to look through his case histories to see how people get screwed over in the pursuit of snack fortunes, even by their own family. So we both vowed to keep the recipe a secret, like Colonel Sanders has with his secret mix of herbs and spices. I suggested I make a note of it and lock it away in the Palace, using Baby Face's briefcase, handcuffed to an immovable object. But HP insisted we commit it to memory and never speak about it again, to each other and definitely not to anybody else.

There was something about father and son, out in the garden, huddled round a warm fire making crisps in a bucket, that brought us closer together. 'King Nicholas Butter Chips,' I thought to myself, visualising the packet that might one day sit on supermarket shelves, alongside all the other greats, such as Kettle Chips, Pringles and Phileas Fogg. Maybe I'd have my face on the front of the packet and write about my life in the Empire on the back, a bit like Phileas Fogg, who wrote of his travels in those letters to his Aunt Agatha.

I think HP was a bit surprised that I'd come up with such a good recipe. He said he might get on to one or two of his old production contacts in Wales to see whether it tickled their taste-buds too. Maybe he'd even get on to his successor back at the firm to see if there might be a bit of start-up funding available, if he fancied the idea.

15

Lord Hills

This man is freed from servile bands,
Of hope to rise, or fear to fall:
Lord of himself, though not of lands,
And having nothing, yet hath all.

SIR HENRY WOTTON (1568–1639)

T he Copeman Empire had had a slightly disorganised and shaky start, but now everything seemed to be coming together and picking up momentum. I had all sorts of interesting projects on the go, with Baby Face and Andrew, and now even HP too. Not all of our ideas worked out straight away – if at all – but then that's the nature of entrepreneurial activity.

Under the banner of the Copeman Empire, everything seemed to have a sense of purpose to it and, when all the revenue streams from our various exploits were added together, they brought in a pretty healthy income, which made a useful addition to the weekly dole cheque, and afforded me all sorts of perks.

As Andrew often says, 'The world is full of money ... you've just got to persuade people to hand it over' and I was working really hard to make a success of things.

The website was coming along nicely and visits were up to around two thousand a month, which, even Andrew had to agree, was pretty good going. When Andrew and I had first set the site up, I'd surfed around the Net, checking out websites to do with royalty and nobility. I'd come across an interesting site for the 'Knights Templar', which was some old religious order that awarded all sorts of titles within the organisation, such as 'Duke', 'Earl' and 'Marquis'. After a bit more surfing, I found several more sites offering all sorts of titles for sale. In fact, it turned out from my research that Prince Edward and Sophie Rhys-Jones themselves have pretty weird titles, because the county of Wessex, of which they're supposed to be Earl and Countess, doesn't actually exist.

Andrew said there was a sucker born every minute and that there were all sorts of people, especially in America, who'd pay good money to acquire a noble title, even if it wasn't really all that noble at all. It might have only cost me twenty-nine quid to change my name by deed poll to King Nicholas, but across the pond, there'd probably be plenty of silly billies who'd happily pay thousands.

We took another look around some of the websites offering titles and Andrew reckoned that most of them looked a bit amateurish, and he was sure he could put something miles better together. And, because we already had a website with all sorts of other stuff on it to do with me and my Empire, people would be more likely to think the titles were legit. Andrew obviously sensed that there could be big bucks involved and said that now the site was moving from being pleasure to business, he'd expect a cut of any profits to reward him for all the work he'd put in. We spent almost an hour negotiating over what percentage he should get, arguing right down to the second decimal place, finally arriving at 42.64%. That's hardball business negotiations for you.

We put some very smart pages on the website, explaining what titles were on offer, how much they cost, and a description of all the perks that could come your way as a result. Andrew suggested that we should make up a few bogus quotes at the bottom to add weight to our claims, and I made some stuff up from pretend Copeman nobility, saying how, since they'd acquired their titles, they'd started getting free flight upgrades, better restaurant seats and invitations to posh parties.

We priced all the titles between two and four thousand pounds, and made the selection procedure look quite stringent – including a questionnaire and the promise of rigorous checks, to ensure that applicants really were who they said they were. Andrew reckoned this would put punters on the back foot and feel like they were the ones under scrutiny, rather than us.

We also gave a proper address for sending enquiries and applications to – my address at the caravan park – but disguised so it sounded like it was an embassy rather than a caravan. Andrew thought it would help reassure people we were a reputable operation.

Almost as soon as we put the pages up and they hit the search engines, we started getting enquiries from people who were obviously shopping around for a title. Most of them were total timewasters and the one or two that seemed to express a genuine interest at first came to nothing.

So we weren't expecting much when we received yet another e-mail, this time from a bloke called Bob Hills, who lived in Acock's Green in Birmingham and wanted to know more about Copeman Lordships.

He started off by asking exactly what he'd get for his money, which was a bit tedious really, because it was all spelt out on the website. Still, I wrote back, pretending to be someone called Lord Chivers, explaining that Copeman Empire Lordships weren't handed out willy nilly to just anyone, and that there was a rigorous selection process to ensure that only applications from candidates who could uphold the standards of the Empire would be admitted. As for the money aspect, that only became an issue if and when his application was approved, whereupon he'd be required to cover a one-off administration fee of £1,999.99, so that the legal documentation could be drawn up and a wax sealer crafted, bearing his initial.

I reassured him that, if he were accepted, and filled in the paperwork correctly, the name change would be recognised by all government agencies, allowing him to get all his documents and records reissued or changed to reflect his new title, including his passport, driving licence, bank accounts and all his credit cards. I knew this was true, of course, because I'd done the same thing myself – just that I'd paid twenty-nine quid, rather than two grand. Andrew tacked on a good bit at the end of my e-mail, pointing out that the real issue at this stage was whether or not Bob would actually be eligible for a title. He said that the Empire was receiving many applications on a daily basis, and that the success rate was very low – around one per cent of applicants. Until Bob had filled out an application form, it would all be hypothetical.

We didn't hear anything from Bob for a few days and I thought we might have scared him off, but then, one morning, an application form arrived in the post.

It was him. Bob had applied.

APPLICATION FOR COPEMAN EMPIRE TITLE
STRICTLY CONFIDENTIAL

Title: Mr
First name: Robert
Middle name(s): John Andrew
Surname: Hills (BSc)
Date of birth: 18.04.44
Address: 14 Leyland Road
Acock's Green, West Midlands
Postcode: B91 2FA
Nationality: British
Occupation: Retired Regional Sales Manager
Annual income: c £18,000 (pension + share dividends)
Clubs: Olton Golf Club, Acock's Green Bowls Club, British
      Legion (Associate Member)
Blood group: A positive
State of health: Very good
Marital status: Married with two children
Name of spouse (if applicable): Mrs Mary Catherine Hills
Name of eldest son (if applicable): Mr Derek Robert Hills
Copeman Empire Title applied for: Lordship

Details of previous professional and recreational achieve-ments and awards:
Apprenticed to a local Birmingham engineering company
(Apprentice of the Year 1961), I qualified in Management and
rose to be supervisor of the packing department. I was
seconded to many working parties before moving abroad
to seek opportunities to further use my broader, strategic
vision. I was headhunted to take charge of a small group of

metal-working companies in rural Zimbabwe, where my no-nonsense management skills were put to good use. Returned to UK because of the political situation and after a brief job in sales decided to take early retirement, to give me time to put something back into society. I recently gained an accredited BSc in Management from Cambridge Hall University (USA) and am planning to gain a PhD in due course.

My hobbies are golf (Vice-Captain: Senior Men's Team: Olton), keeping fit ('Member of the Month' at Flex Gym April 2003), bowls (Club Secretary, Acock's Green Bowls Club), birdwatching, internet and reading.

Reasons for applying for a Copeman Empire Title:
I am a man of the people through and through and I have focused on forging genuine, meaningful relationships with people at grassroots level (both here and abroad), rather than seeking to raise my status through networking with the establishment. I do not regret this for one second, but I do feel it has resulted in my contribution to society being under-appreciated. I feel that a title will enable me to gain a platform to espouse the causes I value, causes, I believe, which are essential to maintaining the fabric of our society. I empathise with the values and cause of the Copeman Empire and, reading the selection criteria, feel I would be an excellent ambassador.

Details of ancestors and/or current relations of note:
Father (John William Hills) 1919–1965. Italian campaign medal in Second World War. Councillor for Birmingham, South (1945–1952). Awarded BEM for political services in Birmingham.

Grandfather (William Derek Hills) 1877–1937. Secretary of Birmingham Baker's Guild 1922–1923; awarded Gold Medal at 1906 Confectionery Exhibition Olympia.

I have read and understood the terms and conditions regarding the issue of Copeman Empire titles. I understand that my application will be subject to rigorous investigation, to establish its authenticity, and that my application may be rejected, without any reason necessarily being given by Copeman Empire authorities.

FOR INTERNAL USE ONLY:
Security Vetting Level: 0 / 1 / 2 / 3 / 4 / 5
Selection Committee Recommendation: Pass / Fail

I couldn't believe it. He'd applied. He'd actually applied. I was all up for dropping the pretence and e-mailing him straight back, telling him that of course his application had been successful and to hurry up and send the money over to us quick. But Andrew insisted that we continue to play it cool. He reckoned Bob would almost certainly be sitting at home worrying whether or not he'd made the grade. All we had to do was maintain the illusion that it was him that needed to be checked out and not us, and we'd be home and dry. So we did nothing until two excruciating days later, when Andrew sent him an e-mail, confirming that his application had been received, but that due to the large number of applications currently being processed his could not be looked at before the next selection committee board meeting, in another three days' time. He signed off the e-mail as 'Andrew Waters', which I thought was a bit of a risk, seeing as it was his real name, but Andrew winked and said that the last thing anyone would expect a con artist to use would be his real name.

Three days later, I had the pleasure of writing to Bob with some great news. The committee had met to consider his application and, after extensive checks into his background, he'd been given full backing and was to receive the title of 'Lord'. The paperwork was now being drawn up, in line with British and Copeman Empire Law, and, upon payment of the £1,999.99 administration charge, the title would be officially conferred to him. As I told him, he really was a very lucky man – 18 other applicants had been turned down at the same selection committee, and he had only narrowly passed himself, thanks to his impressive Birmingham-based heritage.

I reckoned that just sending out a plain deed poll wouldn't be anything like grand enough, so I decided I'd also make a fancy certificate to go with it, so he'd have something posh to hang on the wall.

Back at the Cloisters, over dinner, Baby Face suggested that he could make me a really convincing certificate for fifty notes. I laughed out loud. He obviously knew I was about to rake in some serious dough, and fancied milking it. Still, I felt a bit bad about having left him out of things recently – I'd been spending a lot of time with Andrew, and I think he was feeling a bit unwanted. So, I agreed to let him make me a certificate, but only once I'd negotiated him down to £20, plus a Zinger Tower Meal.

It was well worth paying him so much, because what he made was absolutely brilliant. He'd started off by soaking the back of a Ready Brek box in a baking tray of water, before peeling the printed coating off. Then, once it had dried off a bit, he'd rubbed the surface with an old tea bag, before bunging it in the oven and baking it for a few minutes to give it a really olde worlde look. Then he wrote some grand-sounding stuff on it with a straw that he'd carefully cut to make a quill nib, followed by 'Lord Hills', in big letters at the bottom.

He'd left space for me to sign it, and seal it with my wax sealer, which my Auntie Teresa had bought me for my birthday when I was a kid. In fact, I'd sent off for a new sealer just like it, with an 'H' on the bottom, to send over to Lord Hills, as part of his induction pack.

I signed my name with a flourish: 'Nicholas I'.

I don't know why I added the 'I' after the 'Nicholas'. Baby Face said it looked a bit odd, because, after all, Queen Elizabeth I only started being called that once Queen Elizabeth II came along and by then she was dead anyway.

I think creating my first peer suddenly made me feel a bit philosophical. I'm sure I was getting a touch carried away, but I felt that one day I'd have a son and heir – maybe even with Zara – who'd take over as King when I died. And it'd only be a matter of time before, some time in the future, a new King Nicholas would be crowned, this time 'King Nicholas II', named after me – the one who started it all off.

My wonderful vision of the future was sharply interrupted by Baby Face, who unscrewed the lid off a fresh bottle of Irn-Bru, which must have got badly shaken up at some point, because it sprayed all over the place and made my romper suit very wet on the crotch, so it looked like I'd wet myself. Luckily, and perhaps slightly eerily, the certificate was hardly touched, a bit like that story in the Bible, when that bloke left his fleece outside overnight, and all the ground around it got wet, but the fleece didn't.

I don't remember Andrew ever previously having got remotely excited about anything. But when I went round to visit him, with an envelope that had arrived in the post with a Birmingham postmark, and opened it up to reveal a cheque for £1,999.99, he jumped out of his seat, punched the air several times and started whooping with delight, before charging over to me and giving me a big bear hug that almost made me cough up the cashew nuts I'd been eating on the way over.

16

Trappings of Success

And pomp, and feast, and revelry,
With mask, and antique pageantry,
Such sights as youthful poets dream,
On summer eves by haunted stream.

JOHN MILTON (1608–1674)

I was on the phone to telephone banking, checking that Lord Hills's payment had cleared OK – which it had – and was getting the latest figures from my various equity and foreign exchange trading accounts. I had just finished and was about to say goodbye, when the lady asked whether I could hold on for just one moment, because the system was showing that I was eligible for a low interest rate loan, and might I perhaps be interested? I thought it rather odd that they should think I needed a loan now that I was, for the first time in ages, back into the black, but Andrew later told me that banks are always offering loans to people who have money and hardly ever to people who don't.

The lady said I was eligible for a loan of up to £6,000 and, while I couldn't think of anything pressing I'd need the money for off the top of my head, I figured there could be no harm in getting some further information sent over. After all, if the butter chips really took off, I might need to invest more capital to help develop the business.

Baby Face said I'd been working very hard lately – harder than a lot of people with real jobs – and that I should use the money to treat myself. I was a king after all, and no king should be expected to survive on the cheap. He reckoned it was always a good idea to borrow something when it was on offer, and I should just take the money and run.

So I filled in the form, sent it off and, two days later, I received a letter confirming my new credit facilities. I know it wasn't actually my money, but seeing a six with three zeros after it suddenly made me feel totally loaded. Overnight, I'd come into more money than I'd ever had at my disposal before. I was going to spend, spend, spend.

I know they say money can't buy you happiness, or good taste, and I suppose you've only got to look at Premiership footballers to know that's true. I always felt I had the opposite problem – impeccable taste, but no money. I was always having ideas about the manner in which I'd like to live, but I just lacked the cash to satisfy my appetite. HP always says that if you're successful and have taste then you don't need to flaunt it, which is why he's perfectly happy driving an old Volvo and wearing a plain Casio watch. But Baby Face says you can't take money with you and that if you've got it, spend it. With my new-found wealth, from selling the title, coupled with my big loan from the bank, I was suddenly able to afford the royal lifestyle that I always felt I deserved.

New expenditures, which would at first seem extravagant, would soon become just part of the usual routine. When I was little, I wouldn't get new clothes until the old ones had worn out or I'd grown out of them, but now I began to amass quite a wardrobe.

I started picking up fashion tips in the EDP colour supplement and making regular trips into Norwich to visit TK Maxx for new, though reduced price, designer clothes. I even invested in a new bespoke suit from Mr Green – a very snazzy, closely woven silver-grey woollen one, with 'antique gold' pin-stripes. It cost much more than the blue one because I chose the material from Mr Green's book of exclusive materials. He told me that the fabric I picked out was the same as that which Alan Clark used to wear.

I suppose spending did start to get a bit out of control – Mumsy had always said I had champagne tastes and beer money – and now I was literally popping open bottles of Freixenet for even the slightest occasion – getting the conundrum on *Countdown*, two numbers on the Lottery, or beating Baby Face at Connect 4. And my hedonistic lifestyle didn't stop there.

Baby Face and I were always egging each other on to go one better, and I'd decided it was time that I should get myself some flash royal transportation, so that when I turned up at the Crown on a Friday, people would know His Majesty had arrived. It didn't take long 'til I found what I was after – a Daimler limousine which, though technically a funeral car, was almost exactly the same as the one the Queen Mother used to be driven around in. The funeral driver, Jake, was pretty surprised when I enquired how much it'd cost to hire, not because I was recently bereaved, but because I fancied being chauffeured to the shops and the pub once in a while. Still, a booking was a booking, and he had to agree that I'd probably be more fun than most of the morbid punters he had to drive around at fifteen miles an hour. The only condition was that I wouldn't be allowed to eat anything in the back, because his young nephew once dropped a piece of Cadbury's Wildlife Bar on the back seat, and it got stuck to a mourner's dress and he had pay for an expensive dry-cleaning bill, which was more than the cost of the hire itself.

And to top it all, Jake pointed out that the car had mounting points for diplomatic flags on the bonnet and a diplomatic crest on the roof. I made a booking straight away, for that Friday evening and, at seven o'clock, Jake pulled up outside the Palace. After fitting two of my black and white signal flags to the bonnet and fiddling around with the clamp on the roof before giving up with the wooden crest I'd made for it, Baby Face and I hopped in the back and mixed up some pink gin, as we were driven along the Cromer Road, then down Station Road, towards the Crown. Everyone did a double take as we went past, and I couldn't resist making a gentile wave at two police officers on duty by the clock tower, who must have wondered who these dignitaries were and why they hadn't been warned that we were arriving.

Though they tried to, even Pete Fowls and his rugby mates couldn't hide their astonishment as we pulled up outside the pub and swanned in, wearing our suits and stripy ties, to order Bailey's on ice at the bar.

Unfortunately, the evening was slightly marred when I returned home to discover a couple of pieces of chewing gum stuck to the back of my jacket.

I was really distraught but, luckily, when I called Mr Green the following day, to ask for his advice, he suggested I pop the jacket in the deep-freezer for an hour, which I did, and when I took it out again, the pieces of chewing gum dropped straight off.

One morning, Baby Face and I had been watching a home improvements show, which said that wall stencilling was coming back into fashion and that it was a creative and cost-effective way of giving a room a distinctive look, particular to the tastes and personality of its owner. By the end of the show, the room had indeed undertaken quite a transformation and, I had to agree, the Celtic-influenced potato stamps certainly gave it a very Irish flavour, which the owner, who was from Kilkenny, was chuffed to bits with.

Looking around my Drawing Room, I decided maybe it was time to give my palace a makeover too. Baby Face's brand-spanking-new Cloisters rather showed me up when guests, such as Mumsy, came to visit. Maybe, with a bit of fresh paintwork and a few fixtures and fittings here and there, I could give the place an upgrade to business class. I'd always liked the sitting room that Kavanagh QC had on that legal drama, with burgundy walls and white coving and skirting boards. My caravan didn't have coving or skirting boards, but I suppose there would be nothing stopping me painting a white stripe round the top and bottom of the walls, using masking tape to get a straight line, just like the bloke had done on the home improvements show.

Baby Face said that although my plans were very tasteful, perhaps they might be a little reserved for a monarch. After all, this was my Official Residence, and it really needed to be 'screaming wealth and opulence', like Buckingham Palace. He said that there was no point holding back – why have just one row of potato stamps when I could have ten, and why paint the place in something restrained, like burgundy, when I could do something really explosive and majestic? He reckoned what I needed was a grand Herculean oil painting on the ceiling, like they have in Blenheim Palace. I wasn't convinced, but he drew me a rough layout of what he had in mind, using one of those Bic pens that has four colours in it. The black colour didn't work any more, but even with just blue, red and green, I got the idea.

What he drew was really rather good and, if you held it above your head and squinted with your eyes a bit, you could get some sense of what it might look like, painted in oil on the ceiling. He'd designed it as heaven and hell, with the flames of hell positioned over the microwave, heaven by the door to my bedroom, and in the middle was him, in full Archbishop's dress, the wild winds of eternity swirling about him, a wooden staff in one hand and a KFC Zinger Tower Burger in the other. I commented that it was imaginative and epic in equal measure, but that I was a bit miffed that I didn't feature anywhere. So he drew my face on the head of the staff so it sort of looked like it was carved out of wood. I suppose it was better than nothing.

Baby Face suggested that we visit Felbrigg Hall – a National Trust home a couple of miles outside Sheringham – to get some more inspiration about how toffs design their homes.

I didn't really want to go and visit, because looking round old houses can be a bit boring and if we were after ideas for home improvements, I thought we should go and check out IKEA, which is where Clare got all the furnishings for her flat in London. Still, I'd quite warmed to the idea of having a Herculean fresco in the Palace and agreed to go and take a look round the place with him, to see if it gave us any further ideas. Baby Face wanted us both to dress up, which I wasn't really in the mood for, but he insisted that if we wore our tweed jackets and flat caps, we'd blend in much better with the locals.

Felbrigg is a bit like the set-up Baby Face and I have, though on a much larger scale. It's effectively two bits stuck together – the old bit at the front, which says, 'Gloria Deo in Excelsis' across the parapets, and another newer wing stuck on the side, mainly to house all the valuable books the past owners had collected over the centuries, a bit like the spare room in Baby Face's van, where he keeps his large video collection. As we walked round, I took down notes and drew little sketches in a notebook, and resolved to get some big letter stencils, so I could spray-paint 'Gloria Deo in Excelsis' on the outside of my caravan. It shouldn't cost too much either, seeing as I could use the 'I' and 'E' stencils three times, and the 'S', 'L' and 'O' twice.

Despite my earlier scepticism, I have to say it was all very enjoyable and even Baby Face was behaving himself and show-ing an interest. One of the rooms I really liked was the Grey Room. It was called the Grey Room because it was painted grey. I'd never thought of painting a room grey before and I don't remember ever having seen grey emulsion on sale in B&Q. But the effect, when coupled with the white skirting boards, coving, window sills and fireplace, was very elegant. An old chap who was sitting in a chair in the corner got up and came over to us, and I asked him about the paint, saying I'd be really keen to get some just like it, to paint the walls in my own home. He said that it was actually a very old, lead-based paint, dating back to the 1800s, and that when the Hall was handed over to the Trust, the paintwork was in a terrible state and an expert had to spend nine months restoring it to its original grey glory, using clumps of white bread to rub the grime slowly off the walls. Baby Face nodded at this, as if he were some kind of conservation expert himself.

I noticed that most of the doorways in the Hall actually had two doors – one on either side – swinging in opposite directions. A National Trust guide woman, who was standing nearby, told me that it was for soundproofing. I told her what a good idea I thought it was, and explained that I had a bit of a problem with noise myself, because my next-door neighbour often liked to stay up late, watching his old *Challenge Anneka* videos. I remembered that the interconnecting doorway between the Cloisters and the Palace originally had two doors and I decided I'd refit mine when I got home, to achieve a similar effect.

I was getting some real inspiration and was keen to get as many details jotted down as possible. But I could tell Baby Face was becoming restless and after a while he wandered off, and I saw him striking up conversation with a family who were reading one of the information boards. At least with him out of the way, I could concentrate on doing a sketch of a boar's head that had caught my attention, which was mounted on the wall along with a load of paintings of people hunting and shooting.

I was busy drawing away, when I suddenly sensed that I was being watched, and I looked up to see that Baby Face and his new acquaintances were looking in my direction, from the other side of the room. When I caught Baby Face's eye, he suddenly marched over in my direction, with the family in tow.

They were a funny-looking bunch – all rather overweight, though they did look kind of sporty, because they were all wearing tracksuits and big, white trainers, which squeaked on the woodblock flooring as they waddled along behind Baby Face, whose brogues made a clip-clopping noise as he strode over to me.

The man, who was clearly the dad, seemed really excited to meet me and his baggy cream tracksuit swished about as he shook my hand – so vigorously that my arm felt funny for quite a few moments afterwards. He introduced himself, in a loud American accent, as John Hollweger, and then introduced his wife, son and young daughter, whose names I forget. 'Pleased to meet you, Your Majesty', he said, and then proceeded to tell me how lovely the Hall was and thank you very much for having him.

I didn't have a clue what he was going on about, and must have looked a bit blank, so Baby Face intervened, and said, 'Yes, Your Majesty, I was just telling John here how you like to come down here quite a bit and chat to the visitors.' Then he turned to John and said, 'See what I mean – he's taking some notes on things that need looking at, as we speak.'

It's not that I'm a spoilsport or anything – in fact I like to think I became far more confident and impulsive as my empire developed – but I really wasn't in the mood for playing silly games with Baby Face that morning. He knew I was busy gathering ideas for a serious development project at the Palace – if he was bored, then that was his problem, because I, for one, was finding the whole National Trust experience fascinating. I had business to attend to, and I could do without him pratting about when I was trying to concentrate.

But I didn't want to be rude to John and his family – it wasn't their fault after all – so, trying to be as pleasant as possible, I said that it was indeed the case that I was taking notes on jobs that needed attending to, and that I really should get back to it. Still, it was wonderful to see them, and I hoped they'd enjoy the rest of their visit.

I managed to get away, but only after John insisted that I

sign all their programmes, and have my photo taken with them and Baby Face, standing under the boar's head. John handed his camera to one of the guides – a stocky lady in a blue cable-knit sweater with one of those National Trust souvenir pens on a leash around her neck – who seemed a little puzzled as to what, exactly, was going on.

After the photo, I returned to my sketching, while Baby Face carried on chatting to John and his family. The guide was still hovering around, trying to listen in.

I was just finishing off, and was about to go and tell Baby Face it was time to move on to the next room, when something very odd happened. John took out his wallet and fingered through the back compartment, before handing Baby Face what I was sure was a bank note. Baby Face popped it straight into his jacket pocket and they both shook hands and said goodbye. Then, as Baby Face started walking towards me, John shouted after him, 'Good luck, sir – hey, let's hope it doesn't rain before you get there!'

The guide clearly sensed that something wasn't at all right, and went over to John to speak to him, as Baby Face came clip-clopping towards me, at some speed – his eyes wide, and gesturing anxiously towards the door.

Something was up, and he insisted that we had to leave, right away.

I was really pissed off with having to cut things short, but there was obviously something pretty serious afoot so, rather than confronting him there and then, I followed him as he hurried out of the room, along the hallway and through a door into a courtyard, before nipping through the souvenir shop and back out onto the gravel area next to the car park.

He shouted at me to hurry up, but instead, I stopped dead,

and demanded to know what was going on. After all, we'd had to pay several pounds each to get into the Hall, and we hadn't seen all the rooms yet, let alone had our tea and carrot cake in the Stables Restaurant afterwards, which I'd been really looking forward to. I was still in the middle of telling him off and demanding an explanation, when his eyes suddenly wandered off over my right shoulder and then suddenly opened wide in horror. I turned round to see the distinctive frame of the guide lady from the Hall marching towards us.

I turned back to find Baby Face had already started off towards the car, and I had little choice but to follow him.

We were walking as fast as we could without breaking into a run, and I could hear fast-moving footsteps crunching on the gravel behind us, and getting closer. But by now we were at the car. Baby Face rolled over the bonnet like that guy on *The Dukes of Hazzard*, but he must have fallen awkwardly on the other side, because I heard a dull thump, accompanied by a splash of gravel and quickly followed by him swearing. He got in the car, unlocked the passenger door from the inside and I jumped in, as he fired up the engine, which, for once, started first time.

I was just doing up my seat belt when I turned to see the lady approaching my door and then start knocking on my window, out of breath, and shouting, 'Excuse me?' I pretended the glass was so thick that I couldn't hear her and made an 'I can't hear you' gesture by cupping my ear with my hand. She was obviously quite keen to speak to us, and tried to open the door. But I'd taken to locking all the doors, ever since I saw a case on *Crimewatch* where Nick Ross said a gang had been going around Manchester city centre robbing motorists at traffic lights. This lady certainly wasn't going to get away with the same trick. Baby Face revved the engine, then selected 'Drive' and put his foot down. The powerful V6 engine, which he's always jerking off about, kicked in with a punch and we gathered up a fair bit of speed once he took the handbrake off. We sped off down the lane away from the Hall over several cattle grids that made the small change in his ashtray rattle, then out onto the A148, before heading down Britons Lane towards the caravan park, playing 'What Time is Love?' on the stereo.

Once safely back at Copeman Palace, we had a big argument about what had happened. Baby Face said he was just a bit bored, so had got talking to this family of tourists, and one thing led to another, and he ended up telling them that I was a king and used to be the owner of the Hall, until I sold it off to the National Trust, but that they still let me live there, because I was an expert on all the artefacts.

He'd even told John that we were raising money to repair the roof, which had sprung several leaks – hence the big metal tubs in so many of the rooms upstairs. A guide upstairs had already told us that the tubs were actually for bathing, but John obviously believed Baby Face and, astonishingly, had given him fifty quid towards the roof fund, right there and then.

Baby Face took the note out of his pocket to show me. I'd never seen a fifty-pound note before and I held it in my hands, transfixed by its soft pink colour, and smooth, silky texture. I went into a bit of a daze, but was broken out of it when Baby Face said, 'Well, if you've got such a problem with it all, you won't want to go halves on the spoils then, will you?'

Over the following couple of weeks, I set to work transforming the Palace. I got in all sorts of flash artists' materials, including lots of rather expensive oil paints, and Baby Face got cracking on the Herculean ceiling painting. He worked really hard, and seemed to get a lot of pleasure from doing it, which was just as well, because I wasn't going to pay him for it – keeping him in oil paint was expensive enough. He'd been very good at art at school, and had always dreamt of one day becoming a professional painter, though he quit after he failed to get into the Norwich School of Art and Design.

I got started on the walls, painting them in a grey emulsion that was an exact match of the colour used at Felbrigg Hall, and after Mumsy had helped me hang some dark red, velvety curtains, and some chandeliers that I bought in an antiques shop in Cromer, the place looked absolutely amazing, although I had to leave the doors and windows open for a few days to help get rid of the paint smell, which left the place feeling very cold. HP had been doing a sort-out in the loft back at the bungalow, and had come across several fancy old picture frames, which he let me have, so I could mount my John Miles, Baywatch and Lamborghini Countach posters in them, like works of art.

The big event in November was Baby Face's birthday party, which we spent several weeks preparing for and which was to be the first official engagement to be held in the newly refurbished Copeman Palace.

The party was inspired by an Elton John dinner party that Baby Face had read about in *Hello!* magazine – a no-expense-spared white-tie event. Baby Face started drawing up a guest list, which soon escalated to over fifty people because for each person he invited there were another five or so who'd have to be invited too, so as not to cause offence. Baby Face reckoned we might have to hire out a function room somewhere, to fit everyone in, but even with his trust fund and my loan, things were getting out of hand, so I talked him round to scaling everything back and having a more 'intimate' affair at the Palace. After all, while it'd be great to go to a full-on Elton John Ball, how much greater would it be to go round for supper with Elton in his own home, when it was just him, David Furnish and Liz Hurley in attendance?

Baby Face agreed and said he'd only invite the 'crème'. I was a bit miffed when he said he'd decided to invite Fowlsy and his girlfriend Katy, but decided I could just about put up with him being there – at least it'd give me another chance to show off how well I was doing. He also invited Chris Marshall from Scissorhands, Rob Wolfe (a mutual friend from our school days who now works at Masterfoods and drives an Alfa Romeo 147) and Matthew Curtis, who's a slightly dodgy local lad that Baby Face had started hanging around with a bit, and who had to be kept under close supervision throughout the evening, because he has a reputation for stealing things, especially other people's girlfriends.

I'd assumed that Baby Face was going to invite Andrew, but it turned out that he wasn't. I'm sure Andrew would have declined the invitation anyway, but still, it would have been a nice gesture to at least ask him.

Because we were a bit short of space, Baby Face decided that we should make use of both of the caravans, and we served pre-prandial drinks in the stately surroundings of the Palace, followed by supper in the Cloisters, which was better suited to dining, seeing as it had the proper table and chairs.

The food served on the night was nothing short of a feast. Baby Face is mates with a bloke called Howard, who works as a waiter at the Dormy House Hotel in West Runton, whose carvery enjoys a legendary reputation throughout the local area. Baby Face did a deal with him to get hold of all their leftovers from the lunchtime service and, for fifty pounds, we got half a large Norfolk turkey, one and a half honey roast hams, ten ice-cream tubs containing various salad bar items, and Howard himself, who agreed to carve the meat and be on hand to serve food and drinks to our guests.

Everyone arrived at seven, except Fowlsy and Katy, who obviously thought it was fashionable to be late. Fowlsy kept complaining about having to fork out fifty-three quid at Moss Bross to hire his white tie and tails. At least he'd made the effort – Rob Wolfe, who claimed to be too busy at work to get himself a 'penguin outfit', turned up in a ridiculous white tuxedo, with a red cummerbund. Katy tried to be polite about it by saying it was 'very Roger Moore', but I was really annoyed by his lack of effort, and suggested that, as he'd come dressed like a wine waiter, perhaps he'd be kind enough to top up my glass of Buck's Fizz.

The real highlight of the evening was a string quartet from East Runton, which we'd hired to provide music before and during dinner, playing a selection of Eighties classics, but all in a baroque style. Fowlsy likes to think he's got a good musical ear because he studied GCSE Music, but even he was sat there for some time, munching cheese and pineapple cocktail sticks, and nodding his head and saying how exquisite the music was, until I pointed out that they were actually playing Bros.

Even though Baby Face forced everyone to have seconds, and Matthew Curtis even managed to force down thirds, there was so much meat left over that Baby Face and I were left eating ham sandwiches, ham soup and ham curry for over a week, and Honey got lots of nice cuts in with her usual dog biscuits at dinner time, when I was looking after her at the Palace.

All in all, the party was a great success and, as the Ferrero Rocher circulated in an anti-clockwise direction, I stood up, raised my glass of crème de menthe, and said,

'Ladies and Gentlemen, I propose a toast to the Right Reverand Baby Face, Archbishop of Fantaberry, Leader of the Zinger Faith, loyal servant of the King, and good friend to us all. Happy Birthday Baby Face!'

Everyone said 'Happy Birthday Baby Face!' and swigged their liqueurs in unison.

There was a moment's pause, then, looking round, Baby Face asked where Matthew Curtis had got to. After searching the Cloisters and Palace, we discovered that he'd left early, taking Rob Wolfe's new mobile phone and Bluetooth headset with him.

17

Death in the Family

 was on a real high, but then – like the Intrepid roller-coaster at Thorpe Park, which Andrew tells me reaches 2G in places, like an RAF Tornado on a bombing run – I came crashing back down.

Honey died, at the ripe old age of seventy-seven (in dog years). I was really shocked.

I'd been there with Mumsy when she'd chosen her. She was the most shy of the litter and was sitting in the corner, chewing on a radiator knob. The owner had had to feed her by bottle some of the time, because she couldn't always get to her mother's milk, often being pushed out of the way by her stronger siblings. Mumsy would be paying top dollar for her pedigree retriever, much to HP's annoyance, who felt any old mongrel would do, or rather not do if he had any say in it, which he didn't. He said that if she was going to be paying top whack for a thoroughbred with a fancy kennel name like 'Malfreca Misty Morning', then it really shouldn't be the runt in the corner chewing on the furniture, who couldn't even stand up properly. But both Mumsy and I immediately fell in love with her, even though the first thing she did when we took her home was to chew the knobs off all the radiators, so we couldn't switch the heating on for several weeks, until we got them fixed, at some expense, which irritated HP still further.

On that fateful morning, it was well over an hour before anyone realised she actually was dead, mainly because she didn't do anything much when she was alive anyway. At 6.45 every morning, HP goes into the kitchen, which is where Honey sleeps, to make some tea. While he's brewing up, she yawns, has a stretch, then quietly gets out of her beanbag and walks over to her water bowl, has a quick, slurpy drink, then goes through to the sitting room to lie by the fireplace, which in winter is still warm from the previous night's fire. In summer she goes into the utility room instead, to lie on the tiles, which are nice and cool. It was only when HP came back from his tea in bed, to put the porridge on for himself and Mumsy, that he realised that Honey hadn't moved and hadn't even made any noise when the post-man came, even though she usually goes completely mental when she hears his footsteps on the gravel. He touched her nose and it was dry.

Honey always looked very elegant when she was sleeping, resting her head on one of her front legs, in a pose a bit like Audrey Hepburn, but without the cigarette holder. Now she was asleep for good.

I won't recount Honey's life story. As you might imagine, it was rather dull, and consisted mainly of walks, sleeps, biscuits, water, meat-chunks, woofs, yelps, occasional sneezes, mud baths, leg romps, brushes, wees, poos and pukes. I suppose, in essence, that's what most of our lives come down to in the end, though in my case with a few bags of crisps thrown in.

When Honey died, Mumsy was bound to be upset, and HP should have kept quiet. But he said something very insensitive, about how Honey was just a dog at the end of the day, and he was looking forward to having time to read the EDP in the mornings, now he didn't have to take her up to Pretty Corner for a walk.

Mumsy wept.*

David Wells and Jim Moss popped round with their dog Polo at about ten. They're two local bachelors, in their fifties and

---

*I nicked that sentence from the Bible, by the way. It originally said 'Jesus wept' and is the shortest sentence in the whole book. HP says that if you copy someone else's work, even if it's just two words, you have to get copyright clearance from the rights' owner. The Commander says that, seeing as Jesus has been dead for nearly 2,000 years, there's not much that he, or anyone else, can do about it. Uncle P says that Jesus didn't actually write the Bible, but if he had, I could still be prosecuted by him, because he rose from the dead, and is still alive now, living with God in Heaven and, come the Day of Judgement, he would be well within his rights to take an action against me.

sixties respectively, who clubbed together to buy a bungalow on The Rise and who know Mumsy and HP through the Sally Army. Jim is a retired train conductor from Lancashire, who's always got this mischievous grin, probably because he is very mischievous. David used to work for the Employment Office and is a big music fan, with a record collection that fills the whole of their spare room. He's got four big sets of wooden shelves mounted on castors that he can roll back and forth to get at all his music, a bit like those big rolling shelves they have in old archives. They were both very sad to hear about Honey, and Polo looked rather confused when his best mate didn't hop out of bed to greet him and just lay there, covered from head to tail in a pink blanket.

Jim shook his head, saying, 'Honey died in her sleep. She felt no pain,' and Mumsy nodded appreciatively. I suppose he was right. She just kind of slipped away without any fuss, like my gran, who heated up some milk in the microwave one morning and died before the pinger went.

Honey had served her nation well, strutting over Beeston Bump in her medieval hound coat, exemplifying all that is dignified and classy about royalty. 'Good bitch', as Uncle P used to say, as he patted her on the head. Good bitch indeed. Her death reminded me how fragile life is. That any one of us could go to bed one night and not wake up to see GMTV the next morning.

I took her medieval hound coat from the utility room and went down to the Sheringham laundrette to get it washed, because it ponged a bit, probably from rolling about in some fox poo. I would have given it to Mumsy to clean, but I thought it might have been a bit upsetting for her. Baby Face says some people get very sentimental about that sort of thing, and apparently there's a widow living on The Avenue who left her dead husband's Y-fronts, unwashed, on his bedroom chair for years, because she couldn't bring herself to move them.

Next day, I collected Honey's clean, neatly pressed coat and took it back with me to the Palace, where I hung it up inside, above the main door, as a reminder that life is short, and that every time I went out, I should make the most of things. Otherwise, I might end up dead too, with nothing more than a fancy suit to my name, just like Honey. From now on, if something needed doing, it would have to be done straight away, or during the next commercial break at the very latest.

The Empire would wait for no man, not even its king.

18

On, Copeman, On!

Through the night of doubt and sorrow
Onward goes the pilgrim band,
Singing songs of expectation,
Marching to the promised land.

SABINE BARING-GOULD *(1834–1924)*
TRANSLATION FROM THE DANISH OF B.S. INGEMANN *(1789–1862)*

ooking in the mirror in the Throne Room one evening, I discovered my first grey hairs growing in my temples. When I showed HP, he was quite impressed, and commented that it was around the time his hair began turning grey that his career in the snack industry really started to take off. But Mumsy had been reading an article in one of her magazines about executive stress and said she was worried that I might be overdoing it, with my increasingly hectic lifestyle. She said the article commented on how much prime ministers tended to age, from all the strains of running a country, and she asked whether I was still taking my multivitamin tablets at breakfast time. I reassured her that I wasn't overdoing it – in fact I'd been taking it pretty easy so far – and that success just seemed to come naturally to me, a bit like Richard Branson. I told her that I was eating well – Taste the Difference no less – and that I'd also taken to drinking Yakult along with my Ready Brek each morning, just like Andrew said the City boys do. Mumsy was a bit worried when I mentioned it had bacteria in it, but I told her that they were supposed to be 'friendly bacteria', and that they must be working, because I felt strong, alert and ready for anything.

My King Nicholas Butter Chips had been proving quite hard work in particular. I'd had a word with a few of the landlords around Sheringham and managed to get them stocked at the bar of the Crown, the Shannocks, the Lobster and the Wyndham Arms. HP had made some nice wooden display stands in his shed, with a profile of my face stencilled onto the back so it looked a bit like a head on a stamp. We'd decided to price them at a pound a bag – pretty steep for 25 grams – and the feedback was that quite a few locals had got arsey about the price, and decided to stick with their Walkers. Sales were disappointingly low and HP thought we might stand more chance reaching the A/B/C1 market by stocking them in places like Burnham Market, Holt and Blakeney. Very few of the bars in Burnham 'Upmarket' were willing to sell bar snacks – most of them liked to describe themselves as 'gastro pubs', which made no sense to me, but we managed to get a stand put in the King's Head in Letheringsett (just outside Holt) and another in the White Horse in Blakeney, who both agreed to sell them at £1.25 a pack. The landlord of the White Horse called up after only a few days to say they were going down a treat, and that he needed more stock pretty sharpish, because he'd soon be running out.

HP seemed really impressed by my new sense of motivation and general joie de vivre and was keen to encourage me. Though he was still wanted me to go off to the AIB and join the Navy, even he didn't expect me to stay for life – or for them to be too keen to have me for life either, for that matter – and he was just glad that I was at last showing some interest in the food industry, which he hoped I'd one day join, after a few years' service in the Navy had instilled some real discipline in me.

To reward my efforts, he managed to get us both added to the guest list for a food fair that was coming up at the National Exhibition Centre in Birmingham, which he said would be the perfect place to network and try and gain some support for my new product. I liked the way he called it a 'new product' – it made it sound very businesslike.

We received further details and a couple of name badges in the post, which were really cool, because they said 'King Nicholas Butter Chips' on the bottom, under our names. HP was very excited at the prospect of going round the exhibitions again, just like he did in the old days before he retired. He'd originally hoped to take on a few non-executive directorships locally, which had for some reason fallen through, so I think he was glad of the chance to go and meet up with his old work contacts and show them he was still active. He said we'd need to take some samples along with us to hand out, and he thought it'd be a good idea to get a business proposal together, so we could show potential investors that we meant business.

He wrote some stuff up on his old word processor and I went round to see Andrew, to get it printed up. Andrew laughed his head off when I turned up with a floppy disk, and said, 'What century are you from, man?' He had to dig around in his wardrobe until he managed to find an old computer which had a floppy drive fitted and, once he'd found one, he wired it up to his main machine. He was a bit sniffy about what HP had done, because it was all done in 'Word Perfect', which he said was released around the time of the Battle of Hastings for typing up battle orders. Still, he agreed that the actual content itself was bang on, and once he'd transferred it all to PowerPoint it looked really slick. He'd designed it with loads of cool animated text, but as HP and I wouldn't have a laptop to present it on, we just had to get it printed out instead, which was a bit of a shame. HP put all the sheets in his presentation folder, which flips open and then secures with a strip of Velcro, to form a mini flip-chart. HP said he'd made more successful pitches than he could count on that flip-chart over the years.

Early one morning at the end of November, HP and I hopped into the Volvo and drove over to the NEC for the 36th Annual Food Fair. It was a really productive trip and HP even managed to collar the chief buyer for Waitrose, who really seemed to like the sound of what we were doing, and certainly enjoyed the taste of the crisps we offered him. HP said afterwards that I was perhaps a little too pushy with him – I'd asked outright whether he'd agree to stock us – and that no one makes it big in snacks overnight. Apparently, it's always a slow process: getting feedback, developing the product and then putting the marketing strategy in place. Still, we exchanged business cards with him and he suggested we get in touch in six months time, when things had moved on a bit.

HP bumped into quite a few old faces from his days in the industry, including a nice, slightly tofty bloke called Chris Sutherst, who used to work with HP back at the old firm and was now making quite a name for himself, post-retirement, on the boards of various Midlands-based food and supply companies. While they exchanged war stories and caught up on the latest industry gossip, I decided to go off exploring and try and pick up as many freebies as I could. I used a trolley to stash all the stuff in, which I hid behind one of the stands. I managed to pick up all sorts, including three sweaters, four baseball caps, two family dome tents, a handful of Parker pens and loads of weird crisps and diabetic chocolate.

We both had a really good day, and I was hoping that, what with all this snack business going on, my success on the trading floor and my foray into e-commerce, I might be off the hook as far as joining the Navy was concerned. I sensed that HP might even be softening when, that night, back at the bungalow, we were doing the washing-up together and he dropped the hint that he might like a new tie for Christmas, and maybe I could get him a black and silver stripy one, just like mine.

But in fact, HP had been hearing rumours around town that not everyone thought my empire was strictly above board and, as I finished drying off the last of the glasses, and he poured himself a brandy, he asked me totally frankly where all my money was coming from, and whether I was doing anything illegal. I explained that everything was strictly kosher – I was just part of the dot com generation, where everyone got rich by playing with computers and thinking outside the box. He didn't seem convinced.

In mid-December, the festive spirit was interrupted with a jolt, when a fellow dole claimer, Harvey White, was arrested for benefit fraud and got a two-month custodial sentence. Baby Face knew him much better than I did, but everyone really liked the guy, especially the ladies. He fancied himself as a bit of a toff, even though he wasn't, and actually lived on the council estate with his gran. He used to drive round town in his old Triumph Spitfire, wearing a paisley cravat and playing classical music on the stereo. He always had the roof down, whatever the weather, and Baby Face and I admired his cavalier attitude.

Someone had blown the whistle on Harvey, and his arrest was a real wake-up call to anyone being creative with their state-related finances. I, perhaps more than anyone, started to feel very nervous. I was still signing on at the Job Centre every Monday, but had been flashing the cash a hell of a lot lately, generally living it up in my royal persona.

I decided to quit while I was ahead, before someone decided it was time to take me down a peg or two, and I called up my share-dealing adviser, over at HSBC Head Office in Canary Wharf, to check the state of play on my trading accounts. They were all doing pretty well, especially my futures portfolio, and I decided that now had to be the time to come off the dole and try and fend for myself, without any help from the state. I might have to tone down my extravagant lifestyle and cut back on all the posh microwave meals, but at least I wouldn't get put behind bars, where I'd be lucky to get fed Safeway's Savers.

Baby Face hadn't told anyone at the Job Centre about his secret trust fund and, as long as he didn't do any work on the side, he reckoned he could pretty safely stay signed on, coming up with all sorts of reasons why he couldn't do any of the jobs he was offered. On his records, under religion, he'd ticked

'Other' and, underneath, written 'Zinger'. They have to be really sensitive about people's religious beliefs these days and, as a result, Baby Face could decline any job he didn't fancy, purely on religious grounds, without there being much that the Employment Office could do about it. We decided we'd still keep up the housing benefit wheeze though, because it was so lucrative and Baby Face assured me that, technically, we weren't actually doing anything illegal.

I felt quite nervous striking out on my own, with no obvious safety net, except for the offer of coming home to live with Mumsy and HP if it all went wrong. When I told HP that I was signing off, he was really chuffed. He stood up, shook my hand firmly, made a slight belch (which I think was unintentional) and said, 'Now, you're a man, my son.' Then he went over to the drinks cupboard and poured us both a brandy, which we sipped away at while we watched *The Last of the Summer Wine* – me sitting in his armchair, as a special treat.

When most people sign off at the Job Centre, it's usually because they've managed to get a job at Bernard Matthews, Norwich Union, or doing some random labouring or driving job. So Jane Harley was very surprised when I walked into the Job Centre, dressed in smart chinos, deck shoes and a rather natty Ralph Lauren shirt I'd bought from TK Maxx, and told her, in a loud voice so all the other punters could hear, that I was signing off to become a foreign exchange and futures portfolio director for Universal Exports.

As it turned out, I couldn't have been busier after signing off. Christmas was almost upon us and Baby Face and I had some of our most successful King's Trust collections over the festive period, although we had a run-in with a security guard in the Castle Mall in Norwich and had to run away in order to safeguard our funds. We were still having difficulty keeping our overheads down and, on occasions, I felt Baby Face was taking advantage of the system slightly. One day, he came through to the Palace saying he'd been doing some research and that, according to a survey he'd discovered, the most generous people in Britain were to be found in the village of Silverstone, in Northamptonshire. He suggested that we should head over there at the weekend and see how much money we could collect.

I didn't really fancy such a long and expensive journey, but Baby Face kept going on and on about it, so in the end I gave in and, that Saturday, we drove over in his Scimitar. We took up a position outside the post office with our collection tub and labels, and got settled in for what I'd expected to be a full day's collecting. But Baby Face quickly became restless and, after just under an hour, he looked at his watch and said, 'Oh, that reminds me – don't they have a famous racing track near here? Maybe we should take a quick break and have a look.'

I was very annoyed with him and reminded him that we were charity workers not pleasure-seekers, but he started walking off towards the car, and I was forced to follow, unless I wanted to be left stranded. He reassured me that we wouldn't be long – just that it would be a shame to be so close to the home of British motor racing and not take a look – a bit like travelling all the way to Mecca and not stopping to do a few laps.

I started to get very suspicious when Baby Face produced some handwritten directions from his glovebox and asked me to navigate. It didn't take that Poirot bloke off ITV to guess something was up, when we arrived at the track to find that, 'by pure coincidence', they had a full day's racing just about to start. And it certainly couldn't have been 'by pure coincidence' that Baby

Face had pre-booked two tickets, which were waiting for us at the entrance gate.

I was outraged when he had the cheek to suggest that, as we were, in effect, now on a 'workers' away-day', he should be reimbursed – for the tickets, petrol money and two hot-dogs he later bought – out of King's Trust funds.

I was feeling extra-charitable in the run-up to Christmas, and decided it was time to really put something back into the community. I'd been eating a bar of Dairy Milk and was busy studying the nutritional information, ahead of the New Year's diet that Baby Face and I were planning, when I noticed it had a 'By Appointment' crest printed on the back. I thought it might be cool if I were to issue a few royal warrants of my own to my favourite businesses around town – just to show my appreciation.

Roy Boy was so pleased with the warrant I awarded him that he got his mate, who makes the big laminated signs that local businesses use to advertise all over his trailer caff, to do a big warrant crest to go on the front, to the left of the serving hatch. It looked really cool and Roy later said that quite a few motorists had stopped off because they'd seen the crest and taken it as a seal approval that his food must be top notch, which of course it is. I even got a free upgrade from a normal-size breakfast bap to a large one every time I visited, which made it well worth while.

Chris Marshall at Scissorhands had done a great job on my hair over the years and HP was always very pleased with his beard trims too, so I awarded him a warrant, for 'Follicular Grooming and Coiffeurial Consultation'. Baby Face helped me make him an olde worlde-looking certificate too, which he hung on his wall, just under his photograph of Old Trafford. Every time I came in from then on, he gave me a wet cut for the price of a dry one, and spent several minutes at the end brushing the hair out of my collar.

Issuing warrants seemed to be having its benefits – suddenly I was getting royal treatment wherever my crest was displayed. So I decided to whack them up wherever I could, in the hope of receiving more freebies.

Then I started issuing warrants further afield. Baby Face had been making a lot of improvements to his Reliant Scimitar lately, adding a purple light underneath and all sorts of bits and pieces stuck onto the bodywork, including a spoiler on the boot, made out of a draft excluder flap. Matthew Curtis even showed him a cool trick for making his tyres look extra fat, by taking the wheels off, and refitting them back to front.

I wrote off to Reliant Cars, telling them how much Baby Face loved his Scimitar and about all the modifications he was making, and offering them a warrant. I got a lovely letter back from the managing director, thanking me very much for my letter, graciously accepting the warrant (though explaining that they wouldn't be displaying it on their own stationery) and asking which Scimitar model Baby Face had, because on behalf of Reliant Cars, he'd like to send a small gift as a token of their appreciation. Baby Face was really excited and rang through the details to the MD's secretary straight away and, a few days later, a big box arrived at the Cloisters by CityLink courier, containing a smart walnut and chrome steering wheel.

And to celebrate the success of the Bank of Copeman, I decided to get some commemorative notes and coins made. I called them 'Huffas' and 'Puffas', as a tribute to HP – the Huffas being the equivalent of pounds and the Puffas being the equivalent of pence. I got the coins made by a company in Norwich that usually makes sunbed tokens, and the notes printed south of the border, in Colchester, by a print works that has a special machine for making concert tickets, which worked perfectly for paper money and included a watermark, foil strip and a little hologram that said 'rock' when you looked at it one way and 'roll' when you looked at it the other. The main expense was getting the things designed and set up, but once that was done, they cost almost nothing to run off, so I decided to get thousands, which I stashed in the spare room at the Palace, now renamed 'Fort Knox', because it was the only room in the van that had a lock on the door.

19
Christmas Decorations

Bring him on horseback though the street of the city,
and proclaim before him,
Thus shall it be done to the man
whom the King delighteth to honour.

ESTHER VI:9

nfortunately for Baby Face, the season of goodwill doesn't quite extend as far as him. For the last two years, he's had to spend Christmas Day by himself in his caravan with a Findus Turkey Dinner For One and only the TV for company. His family still didn't want to see him and the previous year, when I invited him round to ours, he irritated HP so much he wouldn't allow him back.

Still, I'd always make a point of going round to see him in the afternoon, to exchange presents and watch *The Snowman*.

That Christmas I received some great presents from the family, mostly on a regal theme, as requested. Mumsy and HP clubbed together to buy me an ex-hire evening suit, so I could dress smartly for banqueting functions at the Palace, such as Chinese Lottery Night, without having to hire. The Commander's present was pinned to the chest – a big silver star, which he told me was, in fact, a Coldstream Guards tin helmet badge.

I'd told Mumsy that I was after a red Zinger-coloured sash, and she'd got hold of some particularly vibrant, crimson satin from John Lewis's in Norwich, which looked really fiery when it caught the light. I had to wear the sash the wrong way round though, so that it covered up the buckle on the right-hand shoulder of my waistcoat, which was one of those weird ones you get from hire places that doesn't have an actual back on it. Clare got me a very nice Pringle sweater, for when I was dressing in smart-casual, which was called a 'Silver Fox', and had grey, light blue and dark blue diamonds all over it. Mumsy said it was far too nice for day-to-day wear, and that I should keep it in my wardrobe at the bungalow, to be brought out on special occasions only.

My godfather, Paul Leigh, bought me a telephone answering machine for the Palace, so I could receive messages when I was either out, taking a snooze, or busy in the Throne Room. Uncle Paul's got a very posh-sounding voice, so I got him to record the greeting message himself. After three rings, he came on the line saying, 'Welcome to Copeman Palace, His Majesty is indisposed at present, but if you'd care to leave a message after the tone, Palace staff will endeavour to attend to your requirements.'

If there were already a few messages on the tape, it took a few seconds for it to fast forward to the new recording position and, while it did so, the machine played Greensleeves on the harpsichord, which I thought rather apt, since it was written by a fellow king, Henry VIII.

I was generous on the present front myself that year, and as well as distributing a load of posh consumables from Larner's of Holt, everyone also got a Parker pen each, which were actually the ones I got at the NEC food fair, though you couldn't tell because I'd rubbed the little logos off with a scourer back at the Palace.

After Christmas lunch, we all watched the Queen's speech and, when the national anthem came on, the Commander stood up. It was quite interesting hearing about what Her Majesty had been up to that year and my thoughts instinctively turned to my own empire.

The day after Boxing Day, we have 'Siddons Day', when Uncle P and his branch of the family come to lunch. My Auntie Sarah (that's his wife, and HP and the Commander's sister) can't make it these days, because she's in a care home, but Uncle P still comes over with my cousin Christopher and his wife Marceline. Marceline is very nice, and some kind of Austrian aristocracy, which HP, in particular, finds very impressive, and he always makes sure she gets a wine glass with no chips in it.

In an act of excessive generosity, I decided that I'd issue royal titles to all the family. As I pointed out, if they'd had to buy them online, they'd have cost well over twenty grand, all in. I'd made some nice certificates which I handed round, and everyone seemed quite impressed, even Clare, though she accidentally left her glass of red wine standing on hers, which left a ring. I'd also had to make up an additional certificate for a bloke in America called Karl Johnson, who, after driving Andrew and me mad with all his bloody questions, had finally sent over an application form and been given the OK for an Earldom. We were just waiting for him to send the money over – a whopping £2,999.

These were the titles I issued to the family – by far the flashest in the Copeman Empire, after mine, of course:

> HRH Midshipman Prince Huffa Puffa, the Duke of
>   Elborough, KZ
> HRH Princess Mumsy, The King Mother, Duchess of
>   Elborough
> HRH Commander Prince Christopher, the Duke of
>   Gwendoline, KZ
> HRH Princess Clare Elizabeth, the Duchess of Polo
> The Right Reverand Baby Face Archbishop of Fantaberry,
>   KZ
> Sir Peter Siddons, KZ
> Sir Andrew Waters, KZ

'KZ' was a new order I made up, called 'Knight of the Zinger', which is a tribute to the KFC Zinger Tower Burger, and comprises the sovereign (me), the Archbishop of Fantaberry, and four knights. Each member represents one of the Zinger Tower Burger elements. The Commander is 'Bun', Sir Peter is 'Chicken Fillet', Baby Face is 'Cheese', HP is 'Lettuce', Andrew is 'Hash Brown' and I am 'Zinger Sauce'. When the Knights of the Zinger Order assemble for their annual ceremony at KFC on the Prince of Wales Road, Norwich, each member adds his respective ingredient, in order, until complete burgers are made for each knight.

In fact, this ceremony is yet to happen, because it proved impossible to get all the knights of the order together at the same time, what with Andrew's work commitments and Sir Peter's disliking for fast food.

As for the dukedoms, I'd named Mumsy and HP 'Elborough' after their bungalow; the Commander 'Gwendoline' after the road his flat is on in Norwich; and Clare 'Polo', after the mints I always used to nick out of her school bag when I was little.

On Siddons Day, we provide our own entertainment – it's a bit like being a Butlin's redcoat, because everyone is expected to be able to put on a smile and do a turn of some sort or other. All of the Siddons are good singers, in fact cousin Christopher was a chorister at King's College, Cambridge, until his voice broke and he went a bit off the boil, around the same time that Aled Jones did.

That year, I decided to present something historical and educational, by staging a knighting ceremony in the sitting room for Uncle P, who had made himself pretty useful to the Empire over the past few months, answering all sorts of obscure questions I kept asking him about royalty throughout the ages, and generally advising on matters of state business.

The Copemanian dubbing ritual is one steeped in tradition, and involved Uncle P kneeling on two Zinger Tower boxes (which I'd put bath sponges inside, so he didn't hurt his knees, which he's always complaining about), while I drew my sword and then touched the flat of the blade gently on each of his shoulders, saying, 'Eggi Kneggight yeggou Seggir Peggetegger, threggough thegge peggowegger veggestegged eggin megge beggy eggalmeggighty Zeggingegger', as I did so. If it weren't for the fact we were in Mumsy and HP's sitting room, it would have looked just like an epic scene from an old film.

No one could call Uncle P an emotional man, but as I proclaimed, 'Arise Sir Peter, Knight of the Zinger Order and Loyal Protector of the King', I detected a slight tear in his eye, which I mentioned to him and which he blamed on dust. He blew his nose, the cold winter sun reflecting on his bald head, and everyone, without prompting, applauded. Sir Peter was visibly moved, shook my hand and said, with a voice cracked with emotion, 'God save the King.'

CLASSIFIED AND RESTRICTED INFORMATION

FOR AUTHORISED PERSONNEL ONLY

DOCUMENTATION PREPARED BY ████████████

Appendix (i) - Theatre of Operation: City suite Ramada Hotel, Norwich

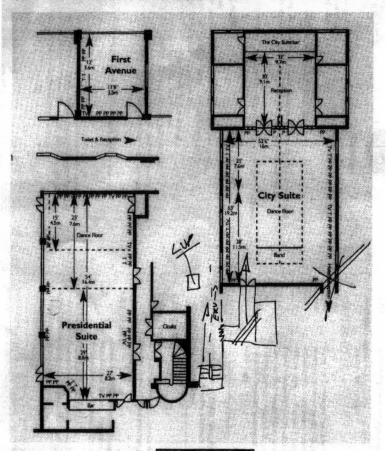

RAMADA JARVIS

Ramada Jarvis Norwich
Boundary Road
Norwich NR3 2BA
Tel: 01603 787260 Fax: 01603 400466
www.ramadajarvis.co.uk

REMEMBER: "Proper Planning and Preparation Prevents Piss Poor Performance"

20
Pride of Norfolk

Like some poor nigh-related guest,
That may not rudely be dismissed;
Yet hath outstay'd his welcome while,
And tells the jest without the smile.
SAMUEL TAYLOR COLERIDGE (1772–1834)

ne idle morning, Baby Face and I were sitting in Copeman Palace, wondering what to do with ourselves. *Trisha* had just finished and it was still over an hour until *Bargain Hunt*. The previous week, we'd held a video marathon by watching all of Baby Face's old *A-Team* VHSs back to back at the Cloisters, until seven the following morning. Baby Face had been getting into jigsaws lately too, and always tried to do each one twice – both the right way up, and then face down, to make it harder. He'd spent several days doing a 1,001 piece jigsaw of Stephenson's *Rocket*, and got right to the end, only to find there was a piece missing. He was furious and said he'd be going down to the charity shop that afternoon to demand that they refund his 50p.

He'd just finished reading that month's edition of *Norfolk* magazine, and chucked it over to me to have a look. He spends ages staring at the society pages in particular, which are a bit like *Hello!* and feature lots of photos of the great and the good of Norfolk at various exclusive events. He says that if you hold the photos right up close, and allow your mind to wander, you can almost imagine you're there. Baby Face often daydreams about what it would be like to get invited to such glitzy-looking bashes but, despite having come up with several scams to try and get his name added to a guest list, he's never yet managed to get an invite.

Andrew says that Norwich is a closed shop and, unless you know someone on the inside personally, you'll never be accepted, which is why he says he has little time for the place, instead preferring to deal with the world outside East Anglia via Internet.

I'm not into going out quite as much as Baby Face and, from my experience socialising in the various drinking establishments of Sheringham, I think there's a lot to be said for enjoying the high quality entertainment you get at home on TV. I am yet to meet anyone in the Crown as funny as the Chuckle Brothers, as clever as Sir Patrick Moore or as good-looking as Melanie Sykes.

Baby Face reckoned that I was just meeting the wrong sorts of people and that if we could somehow get in with the right set in Norwich, things would be different. It was all about being 'in the club', he said. He'd tried to climb the social ladder by joining a few clubs locally, but so far he'd failed to meet anyone at the Sheringham Social Club or the Morley Bowls Club who had the right contacts. He said he wasn't going to be put off, though, and that if no one was going to invite him into the Norwich party scene, then he'd just have to invite himself.

Baby Face decided that on Chinese Lottery Night we should hold a planning meeting, to devise a strategy for getting ourselves into 'society', and he found out information about which events were coming up, and then marked them up on his year planner wall chart.

Top of his hit list was the Pride of Norfolk Awards: a glamorous black-tie event, held every year in the City Suite of the Ramada Norwich Hotel. While there was no disputing the fact that it would be an A-list bash, I felt it was maybe a little ambitious for our first serious engagement and we should perhaps opt for one of the more low key events on his list, such as the Anglian Windows Winter Ball.

But Baby Face insisted that we'd only get one shot at this and, if we were going to be putting a lot of energy into planning and preparation, we needed to be sure the prize was worth the effort.

So the Pride of Norfolk Awards it was.

Next we had to decide how we were going to get ourselves in, and we couldn't agree on this either. Baby Face felt there was no chance of us getting legitimate invitations for anything in advance, because even if we set up an elaborate web of bogus references, the organisers would have plenty of time to check out our credentials and, as the guests were picked by the organisers and not the other way round, we'd stick out like sore thumbs.

He wanted to make a grand entrance and was convinced that we could get in by using nothing more than 'balls and momentum', as he put it. His idea was that we should arrive in the Daimler, driven by Jake as usual, with the diplomatic flags flying. I'd be wearing my tails and sash and he'd be sitting next to me wearing a black suit and shades and carrying a walkie-talkie. Once we'd pulled up outside the front door of the hotel, he'd jump out just ahead of me and bustle me towards the door at speed, clearing the way ahead. He reckoned anyone on the door would naturally assume I was a top VIP and get out of our way, rather than risk getting in trouble for holding us up. And even if they didn't, we'd be hurtling towards them at such a speed, we'd be pretty hard to stop.

'Balls and momentum, mate,' he repeated, hoping I'd agree.

I thought this was a stupid idea and I told him I'd prefer a 'softly, softly' approach, keeping a low profile until we got in and, even then, just gently working the room and schmoozing the punters, without drawing undue attention to ourselves. Baby Face was unconvinced, but I insisted that there was no point going in there and treating it as a big joke, when, if we handled it properly, we could make some good contacts inside and, with any luck, find ways of getting invited to more events. Perhaps we could pretend to be delivery guys and slip in the back way, then take off our overalls to reveal dinner suits. Baby Face said my plan was 'booooring', and that at least using his plan – even if it failed – we'd have had a good bit of fun in the process.

After almost an hour of arguing, it was clear we were getting nowhere. The fact that the bonus ball that week was Number 46, and we had to eat a load of horrible Cointreau chocolates at the same time, did little to ease the situation.

I said I thought we should get Andrew in to help, seeing as he'd know much more about undercover work than either of us and would have a much better chance of getting us in. Baby Face reeled when I suggested this and was very rude about him, but

I was adamant that we needed some fresh and well-informed thinking on the matter and that Andrew was just the man to provide it. We could deal with the issue of whether he actually came along or not later. So I muted the sound on *Casualty* and picked up the phone to ring Andrew at his flat, while Baby Face sat there seething.

Andrew agreed to see me to discuss what I described on the phone only as being 'matters of state'. He said I could come round to his flat now if I wanted, but to get a move on if I did, because he'd be watching the Bruce Lee Night on Sky, which started at ten, and he didn't want any interruptions once it got going. I didn't mention to him I was bringing Baby Face, because I knew he would probably have said no.

Before we went up to see him, I popped into Dave's 2 downstairs and bought a big bag of chips, which I gave to Baby Face to give to Andrew, as a gift, to help break the ice. I pressed the buzzer on Andrew's videophone entry system – making sure Baby Face was out of sight – and he let us in. Andrew didn't seem at all pleased to see Baby Face, despite the chips. Still, he sat in his executive chair, munching away and quietly listening, as I explained what Baby Face and I were up to and asked whether he could help us with a plan. I was sure he'd want to help out.

Andrew didn't say anything straight away, and put down his chips and sat quietly for a few moments with his eyes closed and his fingers on his temples, deep in thought. Baby Face rolled his eyes.

Finally, Andrew looked up and said he'd just visualised the whole mission in his head, and we'd be pleased to know it was a success. Unfortunately, though, he was far too busy getting to grips with BT's new wireless network technology to be 'wasting time playing silly buggers with you pair'.

This was a real let-down. Having Andrew take charge could have made all the difference. But he's one stubborn bastard, and now that he'd said no, it'd be impossible to get him to change his mind. Then Baby Face said, 'Oh well, if you don't think you're up to it ...'

Andrew almost jumped out of his seat, and screwed up his eyes and jabbed his finger at Baby Face, shouting, 'I'm up to it all right, sunshine. I have seen things ... things you will never see.'

So Andrew was in. But on one condition. He said he'd happily run the gig, if only to show Baby Face how the big boys operate, but if he were going to invest a lot of his time and energy in developing a plan, when he could be out earning good money with BT, then there'd have to be something in it for him, above and beyond the satisfaction of a job well done. Not that he was mercenary, of course, but he said that if he could get us in – and we could rest assured that he would – then he wanted a bounty for his trouble.

For a second, I thought he meant the chocolate bar, but he went online and printed out a page from the Silverman's website, which had a photo and some details for a CWC G10 army-issue watch, complete with Tritium markings, whatever they are. It cost a hundred and ten quid, the cheeky bastard.

Baby Face and I were discussing this later, back at the Palace, and Baby Face said he reckoned we were being taken for a ride. But as I pointed out, it was a no win, no fee situation, and that if Andrew really could get us into the Pride of Norfolk Awards, then it'd all be worthwhile. Still, neither of us fancied forking out for his watch – even if we did go halves – so we decided to have a bet to see who'd end up buying the damn thing. I suggested we have a competition to see who could collect the most business cards during the course of the awards because, as well as deciding who'd have to buy the watch, it'd also be a good incentive for making lots of useful new contacts.

In the week running up to the awards, I was starting to have second thoughts about whether hiring Andrew was such a good idea. He told us very little about what he was planning, saying it was all 'need to know'. All he'd told us was to pack our dinner suits and an overnight bag and meet him in Budgens car park just outside the back of Dave's 2 at midday on Saturday, wearing 'smart casual'.

The other problem was that he called me up to say he needed £165 to cover some of the costs involved in his plan. He said he was being perfectly straight with us, and would be happy to account for all expenditures fully at the debriefing, but, for now, the details would be best kept under wraps. Baby Face was convinced we were being scammed, but I trusted Andrew and knew he was just doing his job so, reluctantly, we both paid up.

On D-Day, there was a real sense of excitement at the Palace and Cloisters as we did our last-minute checks before heading round to meet Andrew. Unfortunately, we were a few minutes late because Baby Face had insisted on staying at the Cloisters to catch the Cheeky Girls, who were performing at the end of *CD:UK*. Andrew was annoyed that we were running behind schedule so early on in the mission, and emphasised to us the importance of sticking to the plan, if the operation weren't to be compromised. He also told Baby Face to take his tie off because it was too bright, and reminded us that we needed to avoid attracting attention to ourselves.

'At all times act the grey man,' he said.

We'd be using Andrew's 'transport' to get into Norwich – his BT van – and Baby Face and I tossed a coin to decide who'd get the passenger seat. Luckily, I won, which meant Baby Face had to travel in the back for the forty-minute journey, with our suit bags and holdalls, along with Andrew's various work tools, fibre-optic cabling and computer parts, which kept jabbing into him as we went over bumps in the road, making him yelp.

We stopped off for lunch at KFC on the Prince of Wales Road just before one o'clock where, over Zinger Tower meals, Andrew revealed the initial stages of his master plan.

It turned out that he had actually done a hell of a lot of planning and preparation, and he had a folder bulging with papers to do with the mission. Earlier in the week, he'd phoned up the hotel, pretending to be a businessman, asking for information on their conference facilities. They'd sent over a brochure and some floor plans, which he'd studied to get a feel for the layout. Later that day, he'd gone online and booked a family room as close as possible to where the City Suite was located.

Andrew said we'd head over to the hotel as soon as we'd finished our Zingers, and get ourselves checked in.

We left the van in the hotel car park and Andrew led the way over to reception. It was a really smart-looking hotel with lots of flagpoles outside, which helped give it a dramatic, international appearance. The check-in process went without a hitch and Baby Face and I did exactly as Andrew had instructed us to – melting into the background and not drawing undue attention to ourselves, while he took care of the paperwork.

Up in the room, Andrew got the kettle on, while Baby Face and I squabbled over who was going to get which bed. Andrew must have been a Ramada Hotel veteran, because he'd come well prepared, leaving the tea-making stuff that the hotel had provided on the dressing table, in favour of his own 'brew kit', which comprised a dual-fuel lightweight mountaineering cooker, a carton of fresh milk with a piece of cool-bag gaffer-taped round it, a packet of dark chocolate Hobnobs, a small plastic bag full of PG Tips teabags, a load of sugar sachets and three mugs. He got the Saatchi & Saatchi mug because it was the biggest, I got the Royal Marines one because I was royal, and Baby Face was left with the BT one, which actually turned out to be quite cool, because it had two little coloured strips down the side which changed from blue to red when you put hot drinks in it, in a cunning demonstration of the speed of Broadband as opposed to a standard dial-up connection. Andrew pointed out that the Broadband strip turned red ten times faster than the dial-up one.

Andrew took a seat by the dressing table, and both Baby Face and I sat on the bed nearest, while he explained the next phase of the plan. He said he wanted to take full advantage of the few hours he had left before the event to do a thorough recce of the building, scouting out possible insurgency points for the City Suite. Once he'd tuned in to how the building operated, he'd 'RV' with us back at the room, then brief us fully. I thought this all sounded very professional, but Baby Face kept sniggering.

Andrew said that while he was out recceing the joint it was critical that we remained in the holding area, because he didn't want our faces getting dirty, which Baby Face thought was a pretty ridiculous thing to say, seeing as we were in a posh hotel. Andrew pulled an exasperated-looking face and said it was a military term for keeping a low profile, so there'd be less chance of us being recognised later on – thereby compromising the mission. He told us both to keep our mobiles switched on, but turned to vibrate, and to use the time while he was gone to check we had all our kit ready.

The hours went very quickly up in the room because they had lots of interesting channels on the TV, and we passed our time drinking tea, eating chocolate Hobnobs and watching the shopping channel, which had an infomercial that Baby Face really liked, about the Tuxedo Paint System. It was presented by a bloke with a perma-tan who managed to do some pretty energetic overhead decorating with a roller, without dripping any paint on the smart dinner suit he was wearing. He said it was thanks to the Tuxedo roller's unique paint-loading system. Instead of dunking the roller in a tray of paint, you just poured the paint into the roller's special internal cylinder, and it would seep out through the material sleeve to be rolled onto the wall.

Baby Face said he wished we'd had one when we were decorating my Palace and when he saw that they were offering seven free attachments with the paint roller, for a limited time only, he took down the telephone number and gave them a ring.

Andrew came back from his recce at about six and, after sitting at the dressing table for a few moments to write up some notes, he handed out some Walkers Cheese and Onion Grab Bags from his holdall and we sat down for the final briefing. I let Baby Face eat mine because I couldn't eat anything – I was too excited.

Andrew had brought his MP3 player and mini-speakers with him, and as he delivered his briefing, he played the *Gladiator* soundtrack in the background, which lent a really dramatic ambience to proceedings.

Baby Face and I had by now both changed into our dinner suits. Andrew wasn't impressed. While Baby Face had agreed, reluctantly, to keep a low profile, at least until we were inside the party, he had insisted that he and I couldn't just go and renounce our religious and royal values for the sake of a party, even if it was the Pride of Norfolk Awards. So, while we were both wearing dinner suits, I had my silver star pinned to my chest and he was wearing a dog collar, which he told us he'd got off Andrew Cartmell, who'd stolen it to order from the vestry of St Peter's Church, in exchange for another five two-litre bottles of Tizer. Andrew said it was up to us, but that if we failed to get in because we didn't follow his orders, and drew unnecessary attention to ourselves in the process, then he would still be expecting to get his bounty.

Andrew wasn't wearing a dinner suit himself, and had opted for black trousers and a T-shirt that said 'Security' in big letters on the front. He said his job was just to get us in, and once he had, he'd leave the 'socialising crap' to us and come back to the room to watch *Pulp Fiction* on cable TV and maybe do a bit of work on his laptop. How he could turn down the opportunity of a night with some of the biggest names in Norfolk, after all this effort, I just couldn't understand.

At eight o'clock, after our briefing from Andrew, we were ready for the off. Baby Face and I could barely contain our nerves and Baby Face's legs kept shaking as we sat waiting for Andrew to give the order to go. Baby Face had spent months dreaming about this and, in a few minutes, all being well, we'd be sipping cocktails and munching on vol-au-vents with the very top level of Norfolk society. Andrew was the consummate professional and seemed totally unfazed by the gravity of the situation. He was totally focused on the mission and I knew that if he couldn't get us in, no one could – not even MI5. He looked seriously, first at me, then at Baby Face, then banged his fists together and said, 'Right guys, let's rock 'n' roll.'

We left the room, turned right, and Andrew led us down the corridor, through a glass door and then down some stairs to the ground floor. We didn't pass anyone on the way, and Andrew led us up to a door marked 'Private – Staff Only', then pressed some buttons on a door lock, which, as he told us at the briefing, he'd discovered the code to earlier, by observing one of the staff from outside through his Tasco monocular. The door opened and Baby Face and I followed him through. My leather-soled shoes made quite a bit of noise as we walked down what must have been some kind of service corridor, but I remembered Andrew's instructions to keep moving and look like we were supposed to be there – so I just carried on, regardless. We must have been near a kitchen because we could smell lots of tasty food being cooked and, as we turned down a corridor on the right, we encountered the first signs of life – several waiters coming and going with plates, who turned to look at us as we approached. Andrew said, 'Evening guys,' and they all said hello back and got out of the way to let him march past, with Baby Face and me tucked in right behind.

At the end of the corridor were some double doors and Andrew stopped just before we got to them and turned round to face us and said, in a slightly odd, formal-sounding voice, 'Here we are, gentlemen, straight through these doors. Do have a pleasant evening.'

He gestured for us to go through, which we did, first Baby Face and then me, right behind.

We had arrived. We really had arrived.

aby Face later told me that it reminded him of *The Lion, the Witch and the Wardrobe*, and that it was as if, when we stepped through those doors, we left normal life behind us and were transported into a magical dream world a bit like Narnia, but in this case the Pride of Norfolk Awards in the City Suite of the Ramada Hotel. All around us were the movers and shakers of Norfolk, and it felt like we were two astronauts floating around in a galaxy of stars. It was mesmerising – the glint of jewellery in the subtle light, the flash of smiling teeth, cackles of laughter, the gentle press of the crowd and the delicious smell of pork pies and perfume wafting through the air.

I was snapped out of my trance when Baby Face jabbed me in the ribs and I noticed a waiter marching towards us as if something were wrong. I suddenly panicked – God, had we been rumbled before we'd even got started? But luckily, he only wanted to offer us some sparkling white wine, and we both took a glass from his tray. Baby Face downed his in one, plonked it back down and took a fresh one, smiling at the waiter and belching slightly as he left.

I had to remind myself that we weren't here to mess around. We had a room to work and business cards to collect. Baby Face didn't waste any time, and struck up conversation with a person right next to us – a plump chap in his fifties – and thrust one of his business cards into his hand and asked whether he could have one of his. Baby Face looked rather miffed when he said he didn't have any and snatched his card straight back off him, before moving off to look for another candidate. He'd been worrying beforehand that he might not have got enough cards printed up at the petrol station, and was keen to conserve his ammunition.

I decided to put some distance between myself and Baby Face, and do a circuit of the room to get my bearings. I eased my way through the crowd, heading in the general direction of the stage area, taking care to avoid the main doors, where a lady and a big bloke in a maroon blazer were checking guests' names off a list as they came in.

I caught the eye of a few people as I crossed the room, who nodded and smiled politely. It was all very refined and I took my time walking back across the room towards the buffet table, this time stopping and chatting to anyone who made eye contact. The door-to-door training on Lawson Way really helped, and I felt quite comfortable talking to people, whereas six months ago I'd have felt decidedly awkward.

While I did get to press the flesh with some regional big-timers, such as the cast of Anglia News, the Chief Executive of Eastern Counties Newspaper Group and Mylene Klass of Hear'Say fame, the Pride of Norfolk Awards is, as the programme states, 'A celebration of extraordinary achievements by ordinary people.' If you ask me, this is a bit of a shame because it meant that I kept bumping into nobodies as well, such as firemen and teachers. (There was even a dog on the guest list called Gordon, who saved his owner's life when his house caught fire and he became trapped and unconscious in his bedroom. Gordon barked loudly until the next-door neighbour realised that something must be wrong and went outside and saw smoke, then called the fire brigade and ambulance service, who managed to save Gordon's owner, and Gordon himself, just in time.) It's not that I've got anything against the public services or talented pets; it's just that I felt they got in the way of networking, and I found myself talking to a bloke with a bushy moustache for almost twenty minutes before I realised that he was just the brother of a lady who was getting an award for her work with dyslexic children.

Still, I did meet quite a few interesting people on my rounds, and exchanged cards with those who seemed interested in my Butter Chips and might be able to help in some way. The big highlight was meeting Trisha, who was presenting one of the awards and was there with her young daughter. She was highly in demand, but was kind enough to have a quick chat with me, and admired my silver star. I told her I was a big fan of her show, especially the ones where they do the live DNA and pregnancy tests, and she seemed flattered by the compliment. It was great meeting her face to face – as I pointed out, usually when I watch her I'd be wearing a dressing gown, not a dinner suit. She even offered me some advice on a couple of problems I had – long-distance relationships and living with a hyperactive person. I'd brought a disposable camera with me, and I made a point of getting a photo with her, to go on my mantelpiece back at the Palace.

The actual awards ceremony itself was a bit boring, but luckily it didn't last too long. Afterwards, I went off looking for Baby Face, who I found talking to Julie Reinger, the blonde weather girl off local TV, who he's always had a crush on. He had his hands in his pockets and was spinning some ridiculous yarn about how, as a man of the cloth, he was deprived of the pleasures of beautiful women. She had a fixed smile on her face, and when I indicated to Baby Face that I was heading over to the buffet table, she took the opportunity to move away.

Then, without warning, something very odd happened, which I certainly wasn't expecting. I was reunited with my long-lost twin brother.

Having read *Prima* magazine on more than one occasion, I know that a girl's worst party nightmare is turning up wearing the same dress as someone else, or even worse, turning up in the same dress as someone else and not looking as good in it. For men, though, this doesn't really seem to be an issue, especially at a black-tie event, where the whole point is that all the blokes have to look the same, unless they're serving drinks or are in the band.

So I was totally spooked out, when I turned round to find myself looking at the spitting image of myself, or rather the spitting image of how I might look in fifty years' time. He looked as surprised as I must have done and we both looked one another up and down, unsure what to say. Apart from the fact that he was in his seventies, and holding a glass of sparkling white wine (I was holding a Scotch egg), we looked exactly the same. Swept-back hair, left hand tucked into the jacket pocket and, perhaps most importantly, the thing that had caught both our eyes – we were wearing identical silver stars on our chests. He looked very puzzled. As did I.

It was a very odd situation but, perhaps given a little courage by the wine I'd been drinking, I thrust out my hand and said, 'I'm Nicholas, pleased to meet you', and grinned at him. He looked confused, but shook my hand and introduced himself as Timothy Colman.

A small crowd had gathered around us, clearly intrigued by this chance encounter between two lookalikes with a couple of generations between them. There was an awkward pause, because neither of us seemed to know quite what to say next, but then after a moment or two he cleared his throat and said, 'I hope you don't mind me asking, but that star – how did you come by it?'

I looked down at my chest, then at his, and said, 'Yeah, snap!' before going on to explain that it had been given to me by my uncle.

He said, 'Oh, and who's your uncle?'

Without really thinking, I replied that he was the Duke of Gwendoline. He took a moment to ponder this, sticking out his tongue a little as he did so, no doubt mentally flicking through *Who's Who*, trying to bring to mind who the Duke of Gwendoline was exactly.

While he was doing this, I kept the conversation going by commenting that they were very nice badges. I asked him where he'd got his from. He looked even more puzzled by this, and replied, matter-of-factly, 'The Queen.'

There was a bit of a bustle in the crowd as a blonde lady in her late forties, with bouffant hair and shoulder pads, pushed her way to the front, followed by a plump, sweaty-looking man with a wonky dickie bow and big camera slung round his neck.

She already seemed to know my new friend Timothy, and said hello to him, before turning to me, smiling, fluttering her eyelashes a little, and saying, 'I don't believe we've met before, I'm Johanna Turnbull, Society Editor for *Norfolk* magazine.' I could see Baby Face lurking in the crowd, giving me the thumbs-up. I smiled back at Johanna, shook her lightly by the hand and introduced myself as King Nicholas.

Her eyes first narrowed, but then opened wide as, perhaps sensing that this was one of those society moments that society editors always dream of, she said, 'Would it be all right if we took a photo of the pair of you together, for the magazine?'

'Certainly,' I replied, almost before she'd finished asking the question. I could barely contain my excitement.

And so the plump photographer stepped forward and took a couple of pictures of us, standing side by side, Timothy holding his wine and me holding my Scotch egg, and everyone went 'oh' and 'ah' as if they were watching a fireworks show. The camera must have had a pretty strong flash, because it made my eyes go funny and I suddenly felt a bit giddy. Or maybe I was just momentarily star-struck. My new friend Timothy still seemed a little confused, and started to quiz me about exactly who I was. Johanna Turnbull was listening in, trying to glean some information, and I suddenly felt very uncomfortable. Baby Face had now joined us, which I thought was only going add to the trouble I was in, but luckily, he rather took me by surprise by intervening and saying that he had an urgent message for me that he needed to pass on in private. I just had time to exchange cards with Johanna Turnbull, before he ushered me out into the lobby.

Baby Face said he reckoned there was a good chance I might get my photo into the society pages, and he certainly wasn't going to allow me to spoil an amazing coup like that, by putting my foot in it at the last moment. So we decided to quit while we were ahead and make our way back to our room.

Andrew must have fallen asleep watching the TV because, when we walked in, he was sitting in the armchair with his trousers round his ankles and the remote control in one hand. He woke with a start and waddled off to bed, muttering that we'd postpone the debriefing session until the morning.

Baby Face and I stayed up 'til the early hours, drinking tea and eating a few leftovers from the buffet, which he'd thoughtfully stashed in his dinner jacket pockets. We compared notes about who we'd met at the party and Baby Face was furious when I told him that I'd met Trisha and said I should have found him and introduced him to her. He said that Julie Reinger was even better in the flesh and that he might start writing letters to her, a bit like the ones I wrote to Zara. Neither of us could work out who the old bloke called Timothy was. Baby Face reckoned he must be part of the Colman's mustard dynasty, but seeing as neither of us liked mustard, we weren't all that bothered.

21

Darlings
of Society

It is a glorious thing
To be a pirate king.

THE PIRATES OF PENZANCE, W.S. GILBERT (1836–1911)

hen that month's issue of *Norfolk* magazine came out, I was the talk of the town. Nobody could quite believe it. There I was, slap-bang in the middle of the society pages, in a photo bigger than all the rest, standing alongside my new mate Timothy. The caption underneath the photo stated, matter-of-factly, 'Sir Timothy Colman with King Nicholas'.

Baby Face and I were pretty surprised to see that he was a 'Sir'. At the time I met him, there didn't seem to be anything particularly 'Sirish' about the way he acted. But when I showed

HP the photo he was totally flabbergasted and said, 'My God, do you know who that is?' He marched off to his study and returned a moment later with his copy of *Who's Who* and there, in black and white, was an entry for Sir Timothy Colman, KG, JP, DCL. It turned out that, unlike me, he wasn't just wearing the silver star for fun – he genuinely was a Knight of the Garter, as well as being the Lord Lieutenant of Norfolk and the head of various other organisations throughout the county and beyond. And his wife, Lady Colman, who I don't think was there on the evening, was apparently an extra lady-in-waiting to Princess Alexandra, whatever one of those is. Baby Face reckoned she probably had to hold the remote control.

HP couldn't believe it and started grilling me on how I'd managed to meet him in the first place. I explained that Baby Face and I had just happened to be at the Pride of Norfolk Awards, and just kind of bumped into him. HP wasn't at all convinced by my explanation, and said that people don't just 'bump into' the likes of Sir Timothy Colman.

Mumsy intervened, and told HP to leave me alone. After all, HP had to spend a lifetime in the snack industry before he met a 'Sir', and even that was just a brief handshake, when he won the award for 'Investment Adviser of the Year – Category B Start-up' at the 1993 Eastern Counties' Food Industry Awards. I was only 25 and already I'd met a Knight of the Garter. As far as she was concerned, I'd be marrying Zara Phillips by the end of the year.

As Baby Face and I walked into town that day to get our shopping from Nobby's, we had a new cocksure manner about us. I'd put my suit and stripy tie on and Baby Face was wearing his dog collar, and we strutted down the High Street smiling and saying hello to everyone we passed. Some kids by the clock tower started throwing peanut M&Ms at us, like confetti hailstones, and even a local ruffian, who drove past in his customised Ford Escort and hurled abuse at us, couldn't dampen our spirits.

Most of the senior citizens of Sheringham seemed very impressed, if not a little surprised. For months they'd been hearing tall tales about what I'd been up to, and never really believed them. But now there was proof. I must be King Nicholas after all, because there I was in *Norfolk* magazine, standing next to Sir Timothy Colman – the top dog in the county. We popped into the Salvation Army Charity Shop to see what new lines they had in, and Ethel came up and did a curtsey, then asked me whether I'd sign her copy of *Norfolk* magazine, which she brought out from behind the counter. For a second, I thought she might be joking, but I could see in her eyes that, for her, I was the next best thing to meeting real royalty. In fact, to her, I probably *was* real royalty. I was really very touched.

Baby Face had noticed that on the bottom of the page, it said you could send off for a copy of any of the pictures on the society pages for £70. I decided that if I was going to get asked to sign lots of photos then that'd make a damn good one, but to save money I only sent off for one copy, then got Andrew to scan it into his computer and run off copies on his colour printer, which he only charged me a pound a sheet for – and he could fit four onto each sheet.

And to top it all, I'd won the business card bet with Baby Face. He'd spent the whole evening getting as many as he could, and managed to collect 22, or rather 21, after I insisted that the one he took out of the rack on hotel reception didn't count. I totally thrashed him, by collecting a whopping 36. Baby Face couldn't believe it, because he was sure he was going to win and hadn't seen me collecting all that many cards during the evening. In fact, he was a little suspicious, because a lot of them had old-style telephone numbers on them. But I reassured him that society people were all about heritage, and often left the '1' off their telephone numbers to show they'd been around a long time. He also thought it a little strange that they were almost all from people who worked in the food industry, but I pointed out that the whole point of collecting business cards was that they should be relevant, and that I was looking out for new contacts who might be able to help with my butter chips. He was really unhappy to have lost, but agreed that I'd beaten him fair and square – and got my photo in *Norfolk* magazine to boot – so that afternoon, he called up Silverman's in London to order Andrew's watch.

ℕot everyone around town seemed to want a signed photo. It was now becoming more and more apparent that a lot of people – mainly those around my own age – were really starting to resent me. And it wasn't just Fowlsy and his mates now. It seemed I was getting bad attitude off people I didn't even know. Baby Face said I was just being paranoid, but it seemed that every time I put John Miles on the jukebox in the Crown, it would mysteriously reset itself.

Baby Face and I had been going to the Crown for ages, well before Fowlsy and everyone else claimed to have 'discovered it', soon after the Shannocks got closed down. And since becoming King, drinking at the Crown had seemed even more appropriate – they even flew a royal ensign from the lamppost outside.

But one night, I went to the bar to buy some of my butter chips and found that someone had defaced the display stand, by drawing a big penis on my head and writing 'Fuc' in front of the

'King Nicholas'. Gary said there was nothing he could do about it and, when I came back from the loo to find an unidentified floating object in my glass of pink gin, I decided it was time to find somewhere else to drink.

Everyone still seemed to get on OK with Baby Face for some reason – maybe it was because he wasn't the ringleader – but even he agreed that their treatment of me was pretty harsh, and thought it wouldn't be a bad idea if we took our custom elsewhere for a bit, especially on Friday nights when the Crown could be particularly rowdy.

So we started frequenting the Burlington Hotel, which is further along the promenade, up towards the golf course and, as we sat back in their smart chocolate-varnished armchairs for the first time, and took a sip of our cocktails, we both agreed that we should have visited sooner. The ambience of a smart hotel – an AA three-star one, at that – was much better suited to us now. They even had a bottle of Angostura bitters behind the bar for pink gin, unlike the Crown, where I'd have to buy a glass of plain gin and add a few drops of my own bitters, from an eye dropper that I carried with me in my pocket.

Baby Face was drinking some disgusting concoction with Bailey's and Coke in it, which he said was his own recipe and for which he was trying to come up with a catchy name. I pointed out, quite interestingly I felt, that 'lager' is 'regal' spelt backwards, so if I ever had to come up with my own drink, it'd be called 'Regal Lager'. I started doodling on a bar mat to see if I could design a label, which I was trying to do with the two words looking like a mirror image with a crown on top, but which didn't quite look right the way I'd drawn it.

It was nice being somewhere where we could relax, without being bothered by the hoi polloi. Baby Face said he'd read in

Heat magazine that Prince Harry likes to visit exclusive drinking establishments himself – heading for the VIP area of some place called Chinawhite's in London, rather than risking going down his local Wetherspoons.

As we sat there, sipping on our cocktails and sharing a bag of Cheese Moments, we started planning what we were going to do next. Everything we'd done so far had been one step up from the one before. After all, just a few months ago I'd been sitting at home in Mumsy and HP's bungalow, eating spaghetti shapes on toast. Now I was a king, ruling a successful empire with interests in equity, foreign exchange, snack food development and charity work. I had all the trappings of success too – smart clothes, a place of my own and a chauffeur-driven limo at my beck and call. Baby Face reckoned it was the kind of rags-to-riches story that'd make Shane Richie look like he hadn't undergone all that much of a transformation.

But I still wasn't content. I wanted to up the stakes even further and put more distance between myself and the ordinary people I was so keen to leave behind.

We started thinking about what sorts of things the British Royal Family had at their disposal to impress people with and I jotted down a list, in tiny letters, on the back of a receipt. We were trying to come up with something really big and bold, that would blow the socks off everyone – something so lavish, that *everyone* would have to agree I was major league.

The royal limousine had done the trick the first few times I'd used it, but that was old news now and I needed something even bigger and better to wow people with. We weren't short of ideas – a royal yacht, a private jet, an army – but, while they were all, indeed, big and lavish, they were all way out of my budget.

But then I casually jotted something down that Baby Face immediately seized upon. I couldn't see how it would be any less extravagant than all of the other ideas we'd listed. But Baby Face said he knew differently.

His Majesty King Nicholas and

The Right Reverand Baby Face Archbishop of Fantaberry

request the pleasure of the company of

Peter Fowls esq.

at the official launch of their private carriage

"Zara Reinger"

to be held at Sheringham Popply Line Station

from 7pm on Saturday 14th February

R.S.V.P.
See further
details overleaf

22

Trainspotting

Oh how I long to travel back,
And tread again that ancient track!
That I might once more reach that plain
Where first I left my glorious train.
HENRY VAUGHAN (1622–1695)

o sooner had we come up with our brilliant
new idea than we were both around town
bragging about it to anybody who'd care to
listen, and quite a few who didn't. Apparently,
Fowlsy laughed his head off when he heard
what we were supposed to be up to and said we'd finally lost the
plot. After all, it was one thing tarting up a caravan, getting some
fancy clothes and hiring a funeral limousine once in a while, but
this was just too ridiculous to contemplate.

But a royal train – or a royal carriage if my budget wouldn't
stretch that far – was now top of my list of regal must-have
items, and I would stop at nothing to get it. What's more, Baby

Face said he had the contacts to help make it a reality. All we had to do was come up with the funds.

Though Baby Face fiercely denies that he's a trainspotter, he has, in truth, been into steam trains ever since he was a kid, and is an active volunteer at the Poppy Line steam railway, which has its headquarters at Sheringham Old Station.

They have all sorts of locomotives and carriages, which run along the coastal line between Sheringham and Holt, and prove very popular with the holidaymakers.

Unlike most of the volunteers, Baby Face isn't all that keen on getting his hands dirty running the engines and shovelling coal about, so spends his time working on the entertainments side – co-ordinating various events throughout the year with a woman called Pam, who is the head of marketing.

They have quite a few things on throughout the year, including a 1940s theme day, which Baby Face always dresses up as a brigadier for; a Christmas carol service at Weybourne Station, for which they hire in a foam snow machine; and several murder mystery parties held throughout the year, which Baby Face hosts – one of the best ones being the 'Murder on the Orient Express' one I went to, where Matthew Curtis turned out to be the murderer and hacked a load of guests to pieces with an axe.

Baby Face said they had loads of old carriages rotting away in the sidings in need of renovation, which the trust couldn't afford to carry out. He couldn't be sure, but he reckoned that if we could get the money together, he might be able to convince them to let us have one to do up for ourselves – as a royal carriage.

He arranged for us to go down to the station to meet up with another volunteer called Glen Eccles, who was in charge of all the engines and rolling stock and, that Saturday, we sat on the platform eating bacon butties and discussing our idea. Glen was a nice old boy in his seventies – a stereotypical mechanic-type, with dirty fingernails and a rubbery black train-driver's hat with loads of badges pinned all over it.

I'd half expected to get laughed at when we turned up expressing an interest in buying a carriage. But Glen had no problem with the idea at all – in fact he really rather liked it. He mentioned that they'd had royalty visit the station before – the Earl and Countess of Wessex. I pointed out that that wasn't quite the same as a king and, anyway, Wessex was a made-up place. He laughed at this, gave a slight bow, and said, 'You're right, Your Majesty, this has been a first.'

He showed us round all the disused carriages they had in the sidings, most of which Baby Face was already familiar with, and which Glen said they'd love to get ship-shape in one way or another. One carriage in particular caught my eye – an old wooden-panelled one that Glen told me was an old 1930s 'Gresley'. It had been completely gutted inside and smelt really rank, but Baby Face agreed that there was something special about it, and it didn't take much imagination to see that it could easily be converted into some sort of a royal carriage, with plenty of room for relaxing and entertaining on the move.

When we got down to figures, we were in for a shock. Even though Baby Face qualified for 'mates' rates', so we'd probably be able to get the carriage itself for a peppercorn amount, a lot of work would need to be done to get it to pass Health & Safety, and Glen reckoned we'd be looking at upwards of five grand just to get the carriage fully trackworthy, before we'd even started fitting it out inside.

I was rather taken aback by this and I think Glen must have wondered whether we were really serious about the whole idea, or just daydreaming. He pointed out that if we were serious, then the next step would be for him to raise the matter at a committee meeting, and that he didn't want to be made to look stupid by us changing our minds and pulling out. So he suggested we go away and have a think about it carefully before committing to anything outside our means.

That night, back at the Palace, Baby Face and I held a summit to discuss the matter further and come up with a concrete plan of action. Baby Face said he still had a bit of money sloshing around in his trust fund, but I, on the other hand, was concerned that my rash spending of late might be catching up with me.

I'd stopped looking at my bank statements some time ago, but knew I'd been living the high life and guessed that my loan must be close to running out. I was still hoping to get payment through from Karl Johnson in America, for his earldom, but Andrew said he kept haggling over the price and then stalling. He reckoned we should just tell him to get lost, but I really needed the money and told him to keep negotiating.

Still, I'd bragged to the whole of Sheringham about what we were up to and there was no way I was going to lose face in front of them, so I decided I'd just have to come up with my share of the money, one way or another. It'd be worth it, to see the look on people's faces when we pulled into Sheringham Station aboard our own private carriage. And anyway, I'd had nothing when I started out, so what was the harm in pushing things as far as I could? As Andrew always says, empires are built by taking risks and defying the odds.

So I gave the project my royal seal of approval and, the next day, Baby Face went round to the station to see Glen and tell him that we'd slept on it and had decided we were indeed 100 per cent serious.

The following Thursday evening, Glen was due to discuss our plans at their trust committee meeting. I was starting to get really nervous about what I'd committed to, and was half hoping we'd get turned down. That way I could tell people I was really up for the whole project, but that unfortunately we'd been turned down, so there was nothing I could do about it.

But as it turned out, we got a unanimous thumbs-up, and Glen invited us down to the station a few days later to finalise the details and meet the other volunteers who'd be working on the project. There seemed to be a real buzz surrounding the whole thing – apparently most of the jobs that go on there are basically routine maintenance, so this was something people were getting really excited about. Glen thought the project might even generate a bit of press interest, which both Baby Face and I really liked the sound of.

We finalised the payment terms – two and a half grand up front and the rest on completion – and, once we'd handed over a cheque, we were free to start our work on the interior, which we'd opted to take care of ourselves, according to our own tastes, while Glen and his men started work on the mechanical and exterior renovation.

Baby Face and I wasted no time in brainstorming interior design ideas. Baby Face was keen to put his Tuxedo Paint System to good use on the walls, and was also planning another Herculean ceiling painting – this time of me and him riding on unicorns, with a host of nude Zara Phillips and Julie Reinger angels circling above our heads, eating butter chips.

I hired the services of a local carpenter called Barry, who was a real whizz with MDF and made us a posh drinks bar and dining room table, along with some new internal wall panels, which he scored lines down with a router, so they looked like they were made with real panelling.

Baby Face and I did a best-of-three coin toss, to see who'd get the nasty task of cleaning out the on-board toilet. Unfortunately, I lost, but decided to sub-contract the task to a local cleaner instead.

Baby Face and I both went a bit mad at the Roy's of Wroxham sale – buying lots of fancy cutlery and some nice big china plates, which Andrew helped me apply some little Copeman Empire crests to, using some special transfers that he printed off on his computer.

A local lady called Dory (I think that's how you spell her name), who works Tuesdays at the charity shop, kindly offered to sew neat little 'CE' monograms onto the corners of ten white napkins and ten white hand towels, which Baby Face bought in Be-Wise.

Once the exterior had been patched up and repainted, in juicy 'jam and custard' colours, Glen helped me stick big Copeman Empire crests on to the main doors using printed acetate sheets and a smear of Vaseline, which he said was how the BBC had done it when they'd come to do filming on the line and needed to add emblems to a train, without the hassle and expense of actually getting them painted on for real.

The costs kept escalating as our plans got more and more lavish, and I was starting to get really concerned about my financial position. I'd only set aside £500 for my half of the interior costs and, together, we'd already spent well over a thousand. So I started juggling my funds about, trying to squeeze every last bit of collateral out of the Copeman Empire cash reserves and I put extra pressure on Andrew to shift another title, pronto. I kept pestering HP too – asking him to get on to his contacts and try to source some development funding for the butter chips, which I might then be able to borrow, temporarily, to keep the train project on track.

I got a real shock one morning when I went to the ATM outside HSBC to withdraw some more money, and it rejected the transaction. I asked for my balance to be displayed and, for a split second, I was elated when '£1,983.88 DR' came up on the screen, but then I realised that 'DR' meant debit. The blood drained from my face, as I realised I had less than twenty quid left of my overdraft. I withdrew the last £10, and the machine bleeped as the note rolled out, just like it had done when I withdrew all the other thousands.

I was in a bit of a panic, but I was determined not to be beaten. Most of the bills could be held off until completion and, as long as I put on a brave face, I might be able to convince people nothing was wrong. Baby Face was really excited about the whole project, and I didn't want to let him down – I just hoped that it wouldn't be too long until at least one of my various projects came good.

By now, the end was in sight, and our focus was on making arrangements for a grand launch party. Baby Face and I had a lengthy debate about what we should officially name the carriage. I wanted to call it *Queen Zara*, but Baby Face had his heart set on *Julie Reinger*, who he'd been writing to quite a bit lately. We couldn't agree, and discussions became very heated, with Baby Face even threatening to invoke the Ginger Snap

Clause of 1999 if I didn't go along with his wishes. But after several days of tense talks, we finally managed to compromise, by calling it *Zara Reinger*, and Baby Face went off to Blyth & Wright to get a brass plaque made.

The maiden voyage of the royal carriage was a very glamorous black-tie affair – one of the most memorable evenings Sheringham has witnessed since Stephen Fry performed at the Little Theatre. People still talk about the evening we laid on to this day and, if everyone who *claimed* to have been there truly were, then there would have been several hundred in attendance, rather than the 38 who were, in truth, lucky enough to be invited. I made a point of delivering Fowlsy his invitation by hand – they were very smart 200g engraved card ones from Rounce & Wortley that I'd managed to get 28 days' payment terms on – though in the end, he didn't turn up. We invited both Zara and Julie along but, unfortunately, I heard nothing back from Zara and Baby Face discovered from Julie's PA at *BBC Look East* that she had a prior engagement.

Baby Face seemed to thrive on the pressures of being a professional party organiser and whereas I became quite stressed out by it all – not least because of my money concerns – he sailed through things like it was an episode of *Challenge Anneka*.

He called in all sorts of favours from mates, and mates of mates, and managed to magic all sorts of stuff seemingly out of thin air. Matthew Curtis had a contact specialising in drinks imports from France, who got us a great price on a load of red wine boxes, Freixenet and a brand of gin I'd never heard of.

A local odd-jobs bloke called Jumbo got hold of some red carpet for us, which Baby Face said looked very 'Hollywood', though if you looked closely, it had a paisley pattern on it. Baby Face hired two trumpeters from St Peter's through Andrew

Cartmell, who were instructed to play a loud fanfare when guests of real importance arrived, such as HP and the Commander, and Baby Face also hired a tenor chorister, who was a bit annoyed when he was told that he wasn't actually required to sing – just call out guests' names in a dramatic voice as they arrived.

I just about managed to scrape together enough money to pay for my half of the catering budget – a real feast, comprising twelve KFC Bargain Buckets, four Wall's Vienettas, various tubs of beans and coleslaw and Zinger Tower Burgers for all Knights of the Zinger Order. Howard and a couple of his workmates from the Dormy House Hotel were enlisted to serve the food and drink, and even brought along some fancy metal serving plates, with those big domes on top. The KFC was served to perfection, thanks to an insulated carrying pod that Andrew had been commissioned to design, especially for transporting the food from KFC, without it losing any of its temperature or crispiness. Unfortunately Andrew couldn't attend the party himself, due to work commitments.

Everyone seemed really impressed by what a lavish affair it was, though Cherry Blois-Brook did suggest that the angels painted on the ceiling were perhaps a little raunchy for fine art. Mumsy got quite emotional about it all, and even HP seemed to be enjoying himself – taking full advantage of the free bar.

Glen, in particular, was really chuffed. He'd arranged for Baby Face and me to be interviewed by a couple of train-enthusiast magazines, who came on board to take photos of the celebrations, before looking underneath the carriage with Glen and taking lots of close-up shots of the various mechanical bits and pieces. I'd been on to *Anglia News* in advance, to see if they fancied doing a piece on me and my carriage but unfortunately all of their camera teams were tied up filming their 'Valentine's Season of Love', which included televised marriages from right across the region, so I had to settle for an interview with North Norfolk Radio.

The highlight of the evening came when the carriage was hooked up to the steam engine and we were all taken up to Weybourne and back, on the first of what were to become our regular charters, which Glen had agreed to allow us on the second and fourth Saturday of every month.

Smoke billowed across the platform and the trumpeters blasted out the Copeman Empire national anthem as we slowly pulled out of the station. Black and white flags had been distributed to children on the platform who waved them and cheered. A group of local youths in Burberry baseball caps had come to watch proceedings too and, sadly, they all jeered and gurned as we left, and the waves of well-wishers looking down from the bridge were peppered with tosser signs. But nothing could affect my joy. Baby Face and I stood by the buffet table, surveying the crowd of family and friends, all happily chattering away and excitedly pointing out of the windows as we gathered speed. I took another glug of my pink gin and picked up a chicken drumstick and, at that moment, I felt like I was the King of the World.

23

Black Thursday

I'm tapped out Marv.
American Express got a hitman lookin' for me.
BUD FOX (WALL STREET)

'd achieved my goal, but at what cost?

The official launch of *Zara Reinger* had been a huge success, but now I had two shoeboxes full of unpaid bills, and one of the boxes was the really big one that my Berghaus walking boots came in – so it was actually more like three shoeboxes full.

And then there were the phone calls. For a while, I'd been receiving hoax calls, and despite going ex-directory, I still had to wait almost a year for the old book to go out of circulation. Even then, whoever it was who kept calling and saying disgusting things down the phone would still have my number. I could, of course, have changed the number, but that would have meant getting all my expensive stationery reprinted, or going through it all, crossing out all the numbers on every sheet and writing the new one above it, which would have looked rubbish. And anyway, I relied on my phone for business purposes.

So I kept it diverted to the answering machine and only checked it once or twice a day.

I also started getting messages from Adrian, my bank manager, asking why I hadn't replied to any of his correspondence and telling me it was important that I came in and saw him as soon as possible.

Baby Face and I had organised another party on board *Zara Reinger*, which we'd optimistically entitled 'Ladies' Night'. Matthew Curtis had got us lots of Japanese beer on the cheap, and while I didn't really want him at the actual party, Baby Face recommended that we ask him along, because he reckoned he knew lots of ladies.

But when I turned up at the station earlier in the day to get things set up, I was met by Glen, who seemed really upset. He said he'd phoned several times in the last week, but that it just played 'Greensleeves' at him for several minutes and then cut out. I apologised for the inconvenience and explained that a lot of people had been calling up lately and the tape was probably full, but that I'd take a look at it when I got back.

He said my phone was actually the least of his inconveniences – the real problem was that my final cheque for the carriage had bounced.

I suddenly felt sick.

Jake had pulled up with the limo, which was full of beer and party decorations. I tried to explain to Glen that there must have just been a mix-up at the bank. After all, it wasn't like I was skint or anything, I said, looking over at the limo, which was parked there, gleaming in the sun with its Copeman Empire flags fluttering in the breeze.

Jake started to unload the beer, but Glen said there was no way I was using the carriage again until I settled up. I owed him just over two grand.

So there I was, dressed from head to toe in Ralph Lauren, standing by a chauffeur-driven, luxury limousine. Any passer-by would have thought I was a big shot, but the simple fact was I was broke.

I stood there for some time, staring at the ground, unsure what to say. Glen said he'd have to raise the matter at the next committee meeting, and it would be up to them what action they took. He said he'd trusted me, and that he felt really let down. I felt like a total shit.

Jake stuck the beer back in the limo and I asked him to drive me back to the Palace. Glen watched me leave. He hadn't jumped up and down demanding his money. He'd been as gentle as ever. But I knew I was really in the crap now – I just had to try and salvage what I could.

I remember when Baby Face's dad went bankrupt, back in the early Nineties, and the way people talked about it, it was as if he'd murdered half the town. Everywhere he went, people would whisper behind his back – not saying anything particularly nasty, just, 'There's Barry Painter – he's bankrupt you know.'

His life seemed to go off the rails, and he grew a pigtail and almost divorced his wife. And then Baby Face fell out with him and moved out to his caravan, the day before his eighteenth birthday. I couldn't understand what the big deal was at the time. Baby Face's dad was still driving a Range Rover and living in a brand new Bryant Homes five-bedroom town house – in fact he still is now. But from then on, he was always Bankrupt Barry, but never to his face.

It wasn't long before I knew exactly how he felt. Word soon spread around town that I was in financial difficulty, and the effects were felt almost instantly. My credit facilities at the bar of the Burlington Hotel were withdrawn, Video Scene demanded I pay up all of my outstanding fines immediately and Starlings wouldn't deliver the FT to the Palace any more unless I paid up-front. Luckily, I stopped getting envelopes from the bank, but that was only a temporary pleasure, because a few days later a courier delivered an envelope by hand from a debt collection company, containing a letter telling me that if I didn't start making repayments immediately they would be forced to recover the money, either by seizing my possessions and/or taking me to court.

It was the first time I'd seen the amount I owed in black and white, or rather red and white – £12,653.26. I collapsed on the sofa.

I needed help, but I couldn't bear to turn to HP. If I told him what I'd done, he'd hit the roof. So I decided to ask Andrew for some advice instead.

Andrew had already heard the rumours and when I turned up at his flat he assumed I was there begging for money. Once I managed to convince him I needed his expertise and not his cash, he agreed to help, but I felt he was taking a bit too much glee in my misfortune and, as he opened up all the envelopes with his commando knife and read the contents, he shook his head and tut-tutted, 'Who's been a silly boy then?'

We went through all my paperwork, totting up who was owed what, and on another piece of paper he made a list of all my assets, which didn't come to much. He started going on about how it was always better to be an owner than a renter, and told me that his flat, which he'd bought off Dave for £28,000, five years back, was now worth just over £80,000.

He reckoned that, even if I gutted the royal carriage and sold off the contents of the Palace including my extensive wardrobe of nearly new designer labels, I'd be lucky to get a grand for it all.

I was heartbroken.

He was munching away on a tube of Texas Barbecue Sauce Pringles, and started twittering on about how it was amazing that I should have fallen so far, so fast – a bit like Robert Maxwell, who everyone assumed was loaded, until he fell off his yacht and people got to see the state of his affairs. He said I should have known my limits and stuck to low-level trading.

Andrew was really starting to annoy me now – I'd come to him for some advice and not to be insulted. But I didn't have the energy to fight back.

He carried on, bits of munched-up crisp falling from his mouth: 'Sandbagged me on Bluestar huh? Thought you could teach the teacher a lesson, that the tail can wag the dog? Well, let me clue you in, pal. The ice is melting right underneath your feet. Did you think you could've gotten this far this fast with anyone else? That you'd be out there dicking someone like Darien? Naw ... you'd still be cold-calling widows and dentists tryin' to sell 'em twenty shares of some dog shit stock. I took you in ... a nobody. I opened the doors for you ... showed you how the system works ... the value of information ... how to get it. Fulham Oil, Brant Resources, Geodynamics and this is how you fucking pay me back, you cockroach. I gave you Darien. I gave you your manhood, I gave you everything. You could've been one of the great ones, buddy. I look at you and see myself ... why?'

Like he often does when he's excited, he was rattling off a quote from *Wall Street* – this time a passage from near the end. I knew the next line and, without thinking, replied, 'I don't know. I guess I realised that I'm just Bud Fox ... and as much as I wanted to be Gordon Gekko, I'll always be Bud Fox.'

Then we just sat there for a minute or two, without saying anything. It was totally silent, except for the whirring of Andrew's computer, the drone of traffic out in the street, and the munching sound as he ate his Pringles. It was like Remembrance Day or something – a minute's silence for the dead.

I snapped out of my daze and grabbed all the various letters and bills off his coffee table, and stashed them back in the shoe-boxes. Then I got up and left, without a word.

Outside, life was carrying on as if nothing had happened. Dave was behind the counter serving up fish and chips for people's lunches, Jim Moss was selling the *War Cry* outside Hunt's and Darren was rearranging the classified ad cards in his window. I walked back to the Palace with my shoeboxes under my arms, mulling over that line from *Wall Street*.

I guess I realised that I was just Nick Copeman ... and as much as I wanted to be King Nicholas, I'd always be Nick Copeman.

24

The Crown Revolt

All the King's horses and all the King's men,
Couldn't put Nich'las together again.
'HUMPTY DUMPTY', FROM MS ADDITION TO A COPY OF
MOTHER GOOSE'S MELODY (C. 1803)

pparently, there's a saying in celebrity circles that you should be nice to people on the way up because you'll meet them again on the way down. Unfortunately, I only heard that saying recently.

After Sunday lunch at the bungalow, HP took me to one side, out of earshot of Mumsy and the Commander, who was pouring himself a large brandy, and demanded to know what I'd been up to – he'd been hearing rumours about me around town. I really wanted to tell him I was in trouble, but I just couldn't bear to let him down, so I said it was just the rumour mill getting the wrong end of the stick. He didn't seem at all satisfied, and said that he was going to have to sit down with me properly and discuss what I'd been up to lately, and how I'd suddenly become able to support such an extravagant lifestyle.

Up until recently, I would have sought any opportunity to swagger about in public, but now I didn't want to go out, I just wanted to sit at home, watch TV, and pretend nothing had happened.

Baby Face had always encouraged my wild spending habits, but now he was worried that all the money we'd put into *Zara Reinger* would be for nothing, unless we could make the final payment and get her un-impounded.

And he couldn't bear the thought of being offside with Glen and the rest of the guys at the station. He'd been a volunteer since he was just a kid and was now torn between forking out for the last payment himself and risking putting his own accounts in the red – or losing the carriage and a lot of good friends.

Things understandably became a little awkward around the Palace and Cloisters, but Baby Face was really cool about it all, given the circumstances. Not once did he blame me for the mess I'd got us into, even though I certainly would have, had it been the other way round.

He said it was no good feeling down and looking beaten – I had to come out fighting – acting as if it were business as usual. It had worked for Neil Hamilton, so why shouldn't it work for me?

He said we should be planning a campaign in my defence, and wondered what I thought about issuing a statement, denouncing the accusations against me as lies? He showed me a draft, which he said was based on a statement made by a

Cabinet MP a few years back, after he was falsely accused of taking backhanders.

STATEMENT TO THE PEOPLE
by HM King Nicholas I

I was shocked and disgusted by the very serious allegations made against me this week and I have no hesitation in stating categorically that these allegations are wicked lies.

Here in Sheringham a small element is spreading a cancer in our society today, which I will call the cancer of bent and twisted gossip. The malignant cells of that bent and twisted cancer include those who engage in lies and other instruments of deceit to obtain information for the purposes of a smear story.

They include those who hold grievances or grudges of their own and are prepared to give or sell false testimony about others to further their own bitter agendas. Above all they include those who try to abuse the power of gossip to destroy or denigrate honourable institutions and individuals who have done nothing seriously wrong.

I have done nothing wrong.

I have certainly made my fair share of mistakes in the six-odd months of my life as a king, businessman and socialite, but I am prepared to stand on my record as a decent and honourable one – in Sheringham, Cromer, Norwich and elsewhere – and to defend it before the jury of all fair-minded people.

If it falls to me to start a fight to cut out the cancer of bent and twisted gossip in our town with the simple sword of truth and the trusty shield of Copeman fair play, so be it. I am ready for the fight. The fight against falsehood and those who peddle it.

My fight begins today. Thank you and good day.

HM King Nicholas I
Ruler of the Copeman Empire

It was certainly epic stuff but the truth was I didn't believe it myself. I was the one who'd screwed up, and even if we did go along with Baby Face's plan to stick the statement up on lampposts all over town, there was no changing the fact that I owed thousands of pounds, and had no immediate way of paying it back. A few weeks ago, it'd just have been another stunt we'd have carried out without a second thought, but now, it just seemed pointless.

Baby Face persuaded me to go for a drink at the Burlington one Saturday night and he even paid to hire the limo, because he felt it was important that we keep up appearances.

But we returned to the limo at the end of the evening to find Jake in a real tizz, because as he opened the door to let us in, he discovered that someone had run a key down it. He was really distraught and, though I offered to help him touch it up, the damage was already done. Suddenly he didn't want to drive us any more. He said nothing like that had happened when he'd been doing funeral work, and that was it. He handed me back the stack of CDs which I kept in the back, along with my cocktail shaker, half a bottle of gin and two

Martini glasses, then he got in and drove off, without even saying goodbye.

It all came to a head one Thursday, when Baby Face insisted we go down to the Crown to check out the new *Who Wants to Be a Millionaire?* quiz machine they'd just got installed.

It was the last place in the world I wanted to go – all I ever seemed to get was hassle when I went in there – but Baby Face insisted, and said I was just being paranoid. I made sure we slipped in through the side entrance, though, and I got us a table tucked away in the corner, while Baby Face went to check out the quiz machine. People kept looking in my direction and whispering.

He came back to say the machine was in popular demand, and there were already quite a few coins lined up, but he'd put a quid down for us, so we'd be sure of a go, even if it wasn't for a while. He wanted to go and watch some of the others playing, to get a feel for the machine, but I convinced him that we'd be better out of the way, minding our own business, until it was our turn.

After about thirty minutes, it was our go, and I hesitantly went up to the machine to pop in our pound and got started on our first round – general knowledge. A few blokes gathered round to see how we got on. Blokes often gather round a fruity together – it's all part of male bonding – and Baby Face and I encourage people to help us out on quiz machines, as long as they don't expect to get a share of the winnings. A couple of them seemed to be taking a very close interest – obviously professional gamblers.

Baby Face had got the drinks in – some strange curdled-up yellow things that he'd been raving about, called Snowballs. He said his gran used to like drinking them. I suppose we must have looked quite sophisticated – Baby Face wearing his red hunting jacket and me wearing a polo shirt with my initials stitched on the front – both sipping away on our Snowballs and actually doing quite well on the machine. But as we continued into the sport round, the two blokes nearest were starting to become a bit irritating, the one next to me in particular – a gaunt-looking youth with a whispy moustache, who was wearing an Adidas sweater and a silver neck chain, and smelt very strongly of Lynx Africa deodorant.

He was standing very close – closer than I'd feel comfortable with Zara Phillips on a second date – and then he started coughing. He obviously had a tickly throat, because he was coughing a hell of a lot, and the more he did it, the more it sounded like a rude word beginning with 'c'.

Baby Face looked at me anxiously, then motioned with his eyes, as if to confirm whether or not he was hearing exactly the same as me. I gave a slight nod. We were now halfway through the 'Movies of the Sixties' round, but by now I was feeling distinctly uncomfortable, and I hit the 'quit' button, which made our winnings from the previous few rounds came out with that loud 'chug, chug' noise that games machines always make, so people think you've won hundreds, when you've actually only won a couple of quid. Baby Face looked a bit miffed at this, but I scooped the money out of the tray and turned to leave.

The blokes were standing in our way.

I said 'excuse me', and Mr Moustache just stood there with a devilish smirk on his face and said, 'Off already are we, Your Majesty?'

After a second, they both stood apart and we left through the side door, leading out onto Lifeboat Plain. We started walking up

Gun Street and Baby Face was complaining that there really was no reason to leave – especially as we were doing so well – when suddenly, I caught a whiff of Lynx Africa.

I turned round to see the two guys from the pub. Mr Moustache approached, his neck chain glinting in the street lights. The last thing I remember was him making what, for the split second I saw it coming, seemed very much like a respectful bow. Except he wasn't bowing at all, as I found out all too soon, as his forehead smashed into my face and a wave of pain shot across my cheeks.

Baby Face managed to scarper off, shouting like a lunatic and trying to get some help. When he got back, the blokes had legged it, and he found me staggering around slurring something about how the Polos I was eating tasted a bit odd.

Baby Face had originally planned to have a few drinks, so he'd left the Scimitar in the car park on Cliff Road. But he could see I needed urgent medical attention and legged it up the promenade to fetch it, then drove back and heaved me into the passenger seat. He sped me over to Cromer Hospital, only to find that it doesn't deal with emergencies any more, so he had to take me on to Norwich A&E.

The casualty staff were worried that I might have fractured my skull and rushed me off for a scan, but luckily I was OK. Still, I had a huge lump on my forehead from when I'd been head-butted, six broken teeth from when my jaws had crunched together, and some badly bruised ribs from when I'd been punched and kicked on the ground.

Baby Face called Mumsy and HP, who drove straight over to see me. Mumsy had grabbed a card from the top drawer of the sideboard just as they were leaving, so when they arrived, she presented me with a Christmas card, inside which she'd written

'Get Well Soon'. The nurse said she'd have to keep me in for another night, because I was clearly disorientated and kept asking for the Archbishop of Canterbury.

I was really surprised when Andrew came to visit me. He somehow looked out of context sitting there by my bed, holding a bag of grapes and making polite conversation with Mumsy. Mumsy went off to fetch us some tea and biscuits, and Andrew handed me the bag of grapes and started telling me how things were going on the Web. He told me that HSBC had suspended my share dealing account, but that he'd made sure my last day of trading was a good one. He said he'd given up on Karl Johnson in America ever getting round to sending us a cheque for his title, but that there was some good news, because one of Lord Hills's mates from the golf club had been in touch, asking how busy the selection committee was at the moment, and whether it'd be a good time to make an application for a title of his own.

Any money would come in useful at the moment, and I asked him to keep me posted. After drinking his plastic cup of tea and eating the whole packet of chocolate Hobnobs that Mumsy had bought, Andrew got up to leave – he had to get back to monitor the close of trading, and then he was due in Wells-next-the-Sea, to install a wireless home network for someone.

The next morning, the police were called and came to interview me. The only thing I could remember clearly was the bloke who'd headbutted me, and I gave a pretty detailed description of his moustache, Adidas jumper and silver chain. I also mentioned that I was pretty sure he was wearing Lynx Africa deodorant.

It didn't take long for the police to catch up with the guy who'd assaulted me – a notorious troublemaker from Cromer called David Chapstone. The policeman who went round to his house to arrest him said he couldn't help but laugh when he found a can of Lynx Africa on the window sill in his bedroom.

Chapstone's mate was really shocked by what he'd done and decided to make a statement against him, along with Baby Face's own account of events. The police officer who came to visit me reckoned Chapstone would almost certainly go down for it. He recommended that I sign some forms to apply for criminal injuries compensation too. Normally I would have been chuffed at the idea of some money coming my way, but now, I just didn't care. The story of the attack made the *Sheringham Independent* that weekend too – front page news, no less – but I was in no mood to celebrate.

When I was let out of hospital, Mumsy and HP insisted that I come home where they could keep an eye on me.

HP took me into his study and went through my finances properly with me. It was all still in a total jumble, but HP was used to making sense of accounts, however shambolically presented, from his days in the snack business.

He was shocked how badly in debt I was and he telephoned Adrian at the bank to arrange an appointment for later that afternoon. It reminded me of when I was a kid, and he used to call up the school to get me out of trouble. But I wasn't at school any more – I was twenty-five.

Ironically, getting beaten up could yet turn out to be the best thing that could have happened to me, under the circumstances, because the Criminal Injuries Compensation Authority was going to be looking at my case in the next few weeks, and might award me as much as £3,000 in compensation.

That night, Mumsy and HP sat me down at the table to discuss my options. I could see they were both devastated. HP had spent a lifetime doing business the honest way – his reputation was everything, and I'd shattered it. Mumsy stopped going to coffee mornings at the community centre on Wednesdays – the room fell silent every time she went in.

The pressing issue was money. HP had worked out a debt restructuring plan with Adrian at HSBC – now I needed an income, fast, to start paying the money off. The AIB was just around the corner and, if I could get into the Navy, I could be sure of a regular monthly salary. Mumsy had suggested that she and HP help me out with some of the money they'd put aside for the big holiday they'd been planning, but HP insisted there was no way they were going to miss out on their once-in-a-lifetime cruise down the Nile, which they'd both worked and saved hard for, just to bail me out.

I was totally deflated, but HP said this was not the time to be feeling sorry for myself. I had to pick myself up and go out and earn back what had been lost. The Navy would be just the thing for me now – a good income, a new sense of respect for myself and others, and some much-needed distance put between me and the people of Sheringham, who were clearly sick to the back teeth with me.

I'd have to start by changing my name back. I was still 'Nick Copeman' on the Navy's records, and turning up as 'King Nicholas' certainly wouldn't get me off to the best of starts. So HP allowed me to print off one last deed poll – this time for myself – and I filled it out, with him as the witness. It felt like déja vu as I signed my King Nicholas signature next to my existing name (which didn't have quite the same flourish to it as usual), followed by my 'new' old name – plain old 'Nick Copeman'.

I had been stripped of my title. I was a commoner once more.

Lying in my bed that night, I stared up at the glow-in-the-dark stars on the ceiling. I'd bought them with my pocket money when I was twelve, from Starlings, and though they didn't glow anything like as well as when I'd first bought them, even now they made me feel philosophical as I gazed out into space.

So much had happened in the last few months but now, here I was, back where I started.

Tomorrow I'd go down to the library and find out how kings went about resigning.

And then I'd have to think of a way of breaking the news to Baby Face.

25

Fall of the Copeman Empire

Another year! – another deadly blow!
Another mighty Empire overthrown!
And we are left, or shall be left, alone.
WILLIAM WORDSWORTH (1770–1850)

hadn't seen Baby Face for several days – HP had had
me confined to quarters – so he was really excited to
see me when I turned up at the Cloisters. He ushered
me inside and cracked open a fresh bottle of Irn-Bru
and poured me a mug.

Then he went over to the mantelpiece and picked up a bar
of Dairy Milk, which he said he'd been saving to show to me,

because it was rather unusual and he'd never seen one like it before. It had been wrapped upside down, so that it said 'Dairy Milk' on the flat bottom bit, instead of on the top bit, where it's supposed to be. Once I'd humoured him by making a thorough inspection, he offered to go halves and broke it in two in the way he always does, so he 'accidentally' gets four pieces and I get two. But this time, he gave *me* four pieces.

He picked up a load of scraps of paper off the table, which he'd scrawled all over, and said I'd better make myself comfortable, because he'd got lots of new ideas on the go to make loads of money so we could save the Empire. He handed me the King's Trust collection tub, which was full of money, and he explained that he'd had to go collecting by himself on Saturday, because he'd phoned the bungalow and HP had told him I'd be unavailable for a few days. He'd stood outside Sainsbury's in North Walsham all day, and made just over £50, and he hadn't even had any free lunch or deducted petrol money.

I felt terrible. But there was no way of getting round it. I had to tell him it was over.

I tried to phrase it right, but as soon as I mentioned the word 'abdicate', he suddenly looked absolutely mortified.

'You mean, quit?' he asked, his jaw starting to tremble. He looked just like he did when Mr Loynton received a note from the school secretary during history, and had to take him out into the corridor to break the news to him that his hamster, Shakin' Stevens, had died.

He begged me to reconsider. He said he was even planning to sell his car to raise money to help me out.

I was expecting him to feel let down, but I'd never expected him to be this emotional about it.

I didn't know what to say. I felt like I'd totally betrayed him.

He looked like he might be about to cry, and I didn't want to see that any more than he'd probably want me to, so I put my mug of Irn-Bru down, left my last square of Dairy Milk on the coffee table, and left.

From: Captain D R J Cockhead OBE Royal Navy

ADMIRALTY INTERVIEW BOARD
c/o HMS SULTAN
Military Road, Gosport, Hants PO12 3BY

Tel: (023) 92542112/92542115/92542116
Fax: (023) 92542122
Email: RNRM.OCAREERS.AIB@GTNET.GOV.UK

Mr N H J Copeman   AIB/SE009411
'Elborough'

SHERINGHAM
Norfolk
NR26

16 March 2004

Dear Mr Copeman

I am pleased to confirm that, following your successful appearance at the Admiralty Interview Board on 16 March 2004, your name has been forwarded for consideration at the Selection Board for Naval College Entry on an Initial Commission in the Warfare Branch, which will be held later this month.

You should be aware that the selection process is competitive, and success depends on AIB performance matched against the number of available places at Britannia Royal Naval College for each entry. It also dep........ and official clearances.

........whether or not you have been selected for entry as an ....y 2004.

........tailed summary of your AIB performance to assist ....e future.

........IB, and the best of luck with the outcome of the

ours Sincerely

PRESIDENT OF THE BOARD

26
The Royal Navy

Westminster Abbey or victory!
ADMIRAL LORD NELSON (1758–1805)

donned my blue lounge suit, taking the little silver crown out of the buttonhole. My black and white tie remained on the hanger – Mumsy had bought me a new paisley one from Hunt's. I placed my sports kit, washbag and a spare shirt into an old suitcase, along with my pyjamas.

HP gave me a lift to the main station, to start the long journey down to Gosport. As we passed by the Poppy Line, the *Zara Reinger* was no longer in her siding.

HP shook my hand and said goodbye and, a few minutes later, as the train rattled over the bridge by the common, I looked out of the window to see that he'd parked his car on the grass verge and was waving up to me, like he always does when the Commander is on his way back to Norwich, after visiting for Sunday lunch. I waved back, instinctively using an inverted gherkin jar-opening gesture. Giving up being a king was going to be hard.

Arriving at Portsmouth Harbour, it suddenly dawned on me that the Navy is all about ships and the sea. I know that sounds a bit stupid, but it was only once I saw HMS *Warrior* moored up, then took the short ferry ride through the choppy waters of the harbour over to Gosport, where I'd take a taxi to the AIB, that it really registered what I was letting myself in for – a life at sea. It's not that I got seasick on the ferry – just that I remembered I didn't really like ships and the sea all that much. Apparently, Nelson didn't either and always used to get very seasick. Still, he had quite a reasonable career, so I figured my lack of enthusiasm needn't necessarily hold me back.

Despite its grand-sounding name, the Admiralty Interview Board couldn't be more unlike the place they showed in that ITV drama, *Hornblower*, which both Baby Face and I used to enjoy watching. It's actually housed in a rather drab brick building, comprising an accommodation wing, several exam rooms, a canteen and a social room, which has a pool table and a TV and video, with loads of Falklands War videos on VHS stacked next to it.

They get through about twenty people on every two-day selection, and you're split into groups of four, called 'boards', each headed up by a captain, assisted by a commander, a petty officer, and a public school headmaster, who comes in for the final interview. My board was headed up by Captain Cockhead – his real name – which he pronounced 'Cockud'. Our Petty Officer advised us to pronounce it that way too.

Before joining the AIB, Cockhead was a submarine officer, and he looked very dashing in his navy blue uniform, with four burnished gold bands round his wrists and two rows of medal ribbons on his chest with a pair of gold submariner's dolphins just above them. I'd heard that once you got accepted to go to Dartmouth, you could get a swanky officer's uniform for next to nothing, thanks to a uniform subsidy from the MoD. I made a point of asking Captain Cockhead where he got his uniform from. He said, 'It's most impolite to ask a gentleman his tailor, Gieves.'

I told him my name was actually Copeman and I hoped I hadn't caused any offence by asking. For some reason, he seemed to wince when I said this, and took out a fountain pen and a small leather-bound notebook from his pocket and made a quick note about something, before walking off.

The Petty Officer later told me that 'Gieves' was a tailor on Savile Row, where many officers had their uniforms and suits made. He also told me not to speak to the Captain unless spoken to, especially if I was going to talk shit.

About half of the applicants pass the AIB and the tests are a mixture of physical and academic. The main physical tests were a selection of *It's a Knockout*-style games, where you had to cross a crocodile-infested swamp safely, using benches, boxes, drums and ropes. They didn't have a real crocodile-infested swamp, so they used a load of blue gym mats instead. I actually would have preferred crocodiles, because I have a real phobia of blue gym mats, dating back to school PE lessons as a seven-year-old. I can still picture Mrs Instone, towering over me in her red Ronhill Tracksters and paisley neck-scarf, screaming at me to do a proper somersault. To this day, the sight of blue gym mats and those benches with hooks on the end brings me out in a cold sweat.

I wished I'd done more physical training prior to attending the AIB, and it soon became clear that I hadn't developed sufficient upper-body strength as a result of my day-to-day activities back in Sheringham. Still, as the oldest recruit on my board, I was automatically appointed leader, and I decided to compensate for my lack of physical prowess by taking care of team strategy – a bit like Hannibal off the A-Team, who was never all that fast on his feet, but always came up with a brilliant plan that saved the day.

Unfortunately, few of my hands-off leadership skills worked, earning my board the distinction of being the only one in the instructors' memory ever to have failed all six tasks. On the one task where they had a real tank of water instead of blue mats, we all fell in, along with two nuclear warheads, simulated by ice cream tubs filled with stones. Apparently that only happens once in a blue moon, because the task is supposed to be extra easy and is there as a confidence booster. Cockhead got very annoyed and drew a big line through my marking sheet and wrote 'ZERO' on it in big letters. He then came over to me and said, 'You foolio', in a posh accent. I assume that's just a flash way of saying 'you fool' – maybe it indicates you're well travelled or something.

Luckily, I fared somewhat better when it came to the written stuff, mainly thanks to HP's tuition, and the headmaster on the board seemed to quite like me during our informal chat. He asked me to name a local place of interest I'd take him to visit, if he were to come and stay with me in North Norfolk. I said I'd take him for a pint at the Nelson Arms in Burnham Thorpe, which is the village where Admiral Nelson was born. Then I asked when he was coming to stay, because I'd need to ask Mumsy to make up the spare room. He must have been quite a sentimental old duffer because, in the debriefing, he said he was very touched by my kind offer.

In the social room, I bumped into some guys who were applying for the Fleet Air Arm, where they get to fly helicopters and those planes that take off and land vertically. I'd applied for Warfare, where you shoot missiles and torpedoes from the ship instead. Fleet Air Arm selection was just the same as Warfare, except they also had to go off and play Space Invaders and a *Countdown*-type game, simultaneously, to check their reflexes, hand-to-eye co-ordination and 'ability to process multiple information sources'. There were also two Royal Marines applicants in attendance, who the Petty Officer said also had to go off and do a hundred sit-ups, press-ups, pull-ups and tug-offs. Someone asked what tug-offs were. The Petty Officer said it was a special exercise that the Marines were always doing, and that they prided themselves on being the best in the Armed Forces.

On the afternoon of the final day, I went in to see Captain Cockhead for my final debriefing. As soon as I sat down, I knew I'd failed, because his first words to me were, 'Copeman, to be perfectly frank, I wouldn't like you in my Navy and I have to say, your Tony Blair mannerisms have become increasingly irritating to me during the course of this selection process.'

I was devastated.

Cockhead shifted in his chair and slowly drew breath through his teeth. He looked down at his papers, then up at me again. He sighed, and then said that, unfortunately, the final decision wasn't up to him – it was down to the score. And though he remained sure that the Royal Navy wasn't for me, the system obviously thought it knew better.

I'd passed, with a score of 500 – the absolute minimum required.

I was ecstatic, and took the opportunity of thanking Captain Cockhead for having me at the AIB, deliberately stressing 'cock' and 'head', which made him wince. Outside, the Petty Officer, who must have already known I'd passed, saluted me and said, 'Congratulations, Sir.'

It was the proudest moment of my life, apart from setting the two-widths' swimming record in J1, which still stands to this day.

The Petty Officer said that, as I'd passed, I'd need to stay overnight and take a medical the following morning. And this evening, I'd be taking my dinner in the wardroom along with the other successful candidates and all of the regular officers. I went straight off to find a phone and tell HP. There was a long pause after I told him the good news and, when he did speak again, it didn't sound like his usual voice. He sounded a bit croaky, and all he managed to say was 'Well done ... well done.'

That evening, I went into the wardroom bar, determined to do my best to blend in. I steered clear of Captain Cockhead and ordered a pink gin from one of the stewards. But as I did so, the officers around me suddenly fell silent. This rather threw me. I presumed they were admiring that such a young recruit had already grasped the finer details of naval etiquette. So I was a little surprised, therefore, by the Lieutenant Commander standing nearby who said 'Arse' under his breath. After a few awkward moments, everyone returned to their conversations and the steward arrived with my drink.

At dinner, I was seated next to another successful candidate – a very camp chap called 'Gucci' – who was currently in the TA, but wanted to go regular as an officer in Royal Naval Supply – one of the few military units that will still commission you as an officer in your thirties. The petty officers had been taking the mick out of his lah-di-dah mannerisms towards the beginning of selection, until they found out that he was currently serving in 21 SAS. At the Interview Board, everyone had been asked, 'How would you feel about killing someone?' but Gucci said they didn't ask him, for some reason.

In fact, the following day, Gucci failed to get into the Royal Naval College, because when they tested his hearing at the medical, his right ear scored 6 and his left ear scored 4. You had to score at least 5 in each. It turned out he'd damaged his left ear firing his sub-machine gun without earplugs.

I passed all the hearing tests and had some blood taken, then we all got taken in a minibus to the local optician to get our eyesight tested, and – accidentally letting my act slip for a moment – I found myself asking for details of a monocle that they had in a display case, which I thought had a rather regal air about it.

I didn't need it, because my eyes were given the OK.

The last form was ticked and stamped. I'd made it. I was going to be an officer in Her Majesty's Royal Navy.

27
The King Is Dead

Here lies a great and mighty king
Whose promise none relies on;
He never said a foolish thing,
Nor ever did a wise one.

JOHN WILMOT, EARL OF ROCHESTER (1647–1680)

When I got back to the bungalow, the mood had changed. There was hope. Mumsy had made sweet and sour chicken for dinner – my favourite – and for pudding there was a chocolate cake, which she'd baked especially, and wonkily iced 'Leftenant Copeman' around the edge. HP had made me a big glass of pink gin before dinner – something he'd never done before – and we sat by the patio window looking out over the back yard, like two naval officers sitting on the bridge of a destroyer, gazing out across the Atlantic.

There was still a slight tension in the air – these weren't the circumstances in which they'd imagined me joining the Navy, after all – but things were looking up.

The next day, Mumsy helped me clear out my stuff from the Palace. I hadn't been back since I'd been beaten up, and I'd hardly spoken to Baby Face either, since I told him that HP didn't want me hanging out with him any more. Opening the door to the Palace, it was like opening up a time capsule – everything was just where I'd left it, several weeks before. Musmy was appalled by the state of the place. Even the majestic ceiling painting and velvet curtains couldn't distract you from the sheer mess of empty pizza boxes, Chinese takeaway tubs and unwashed clothes strewn all over the floor.

We set about going through all the stuff, separating it into rubbish and things worth keeping. Going through all my kingly possessions felt rather strange, and as my romper suit, crown, cloak and all the other mugubbins got packed up in a load of old apple boxes that Mumsy had got from Morrison's, I felt part of me was getting packed up in the boxes too.

Baby Face must have heard us moving around next door, because I looked up to see him standing at the threshold of the interconnecting door, wearing his dressing gown, silently watching what I was doing. I smiled and said hello, but he just stood there looking vacant, like a lost kid. Then he mumbled something about *Beat the Nation* being on, and went back through to the Cloisters, closing the door behind him. I heard a key turn in the lock.

t took the whole of the rest of the day for Mumsy and me to do all the clearing up and it was dark outside by the time we'd finished. HP came round in the Volvo and we loaded up the back with all the boxes and bin bags. They both drove back to the bungalow, but I said I'd hang about for a bit, just to do a last scout round for anything we'd missed. HP lent me his screwdriver so I could unscrew the 'Copeman Palace' plaque from next to the door, because he said it was a nice piece of brass and could come in useful for something else.

There was still a bit of time left on the electricity meter, so I put the small light on in the Drawing Room and sat there, just thinking to myself about this and that. In the background, I could hear the muffled sound of the TV from the Cloisters, and could smell him cooking up sweet and sour noodles.

A framed picture of Zara, which used to sit on my bedside table, now rested on top of a pile of my last effects, packed up in an apple box. I picked her up, took her in my hands and gazed into her eyes, one last time.

Plot 65B (formerly Copeman Palace)
Beeston Regis Caravan Park
Sheringham
North Norfolk NR25 5GH

Miss Zara Anne Elizabeth Phillips
c/o Gatcombe Park
Minchinhampton
Stroud, Gloucestershire GL6 9AT

Dearest Zara,

This is one of the hardest letters I have ever had to write.
I feel you now know me better than any girl I have ever

met, even though, technically, I have never actually met you. You have been with me through the bad times and the good. You knew me when I was a nobody, you knew me when I was King, and now, as I described so painfully in my last letter to you, I am King no more.

The Palace now lies empty. The corridors of power, that once hustled and bustled, are deserted. All phones are set to silent, no faxes whir, no e-mails ping.

The smell of warm noodles brings memories flooding back – of times spent laughing and embracing, as if life would never end. But now the dream is gone, and all we have are memories.

Tomorrow, I must leave for the Navy. I know not my fate. But I must face what comes, and do my best to be brave – not for Queen and Country – but for you and me, and others that I hold dear.

I will never forget you, Zara. Thank you for helping me through.

Nicholas

Sub Lieutenant Nicholas HJ Copeman RN

COPEMAN EMPIRE

5th April

Dearest Zara,

This is one of the hardest letters I have ever had to write.
I feel you now know me better than any girl I have ever met,
even though, technically, I have never actually met you. You
have been with me through the bad times and the good.
You knew me when I was a nobody, you knew me when I
was king, and now, as I described so painfully in my last letter
to you, I am king no more.

    The Palace now lies empty. The corridors of power,
that once hustled and bustled, are deserted. All phones
are set to silent, no faxes whir, no e-mails ping.

    The smell of warm noodles brings memories flooding
back — of time spent laughing and embracing, as if life would
never end. But now the dream is gone, and all we have are
memories.

    Tomorrow, I must leave for the Navy. I know not my fate.
But I must face what comes and do my best to be brave — not for
Queen and Country — but for you, me, and others that I hold dear.

I will never forget you Zara.

Thank you for helping me through.

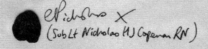

eNicholas X
(Sub Lt Nicholas H J Copeman RN)

COPEMAN PALACE · BEESTON REGIS CARAVAN PARK · SHERINGHAM · NORTH NORFOLK · NR26 5GH

. NO LONGER AT THIS ADDRESS

Epilogue

ife in Sheringham has returned to normal since King Nicholas abdicated and the Copeman Empire was dissolved. Many seem happy to have seen the back of the regime, but in some small ways 'England's other monarch' continues to reign in the hearts and minds of those who really believed in him, and even some who didn't.

Andrew Waters still works for BT. He recently provided telephone support to a Mr James Williams of Leamington Spa, helping him set up his BT Home Network 1250 Wireless Router. Mr Williams was so impressed by the professional service he received from Andrew, that he asked him to become godfather to his newly born daughter, Holly. Andrew accepted, and will be travelling to Leamington at the end of the month to meet Mr and Mrs Williams, and Holly, for the first time, before attending the baptism service. Andrew continues to trade in equity, futures and foreign exchange in his spare time.

At the close of Empire business, two lords, an earl and a

knight were created. The second lord to be appointed was Lord Swain – a friend of Lord Hills and a fellow member of Olton Golf Club. The Earldom was sold to Karl Johnson in America, who, after months of stalling, finally decided to pay up the full amount – £2,999.99. The knighthood was sold as a barmitzvah present for a thirteen-year-old boy living in Golders Green, London. He is believed to be the youngest person in the world ever to be knighted.

Baby Face still lives in the Cloisters on Beeston Regis Caravan Park. He sold off the former Copeman Palace to the Oak Dale holiday park in Ross-shire, Scotland. It is available for hire, from £110 per week – duvets and pillows supplied, pets by arrangement only (see www.kingnicholas.com/palace for more details). Baby Face recently traded his Reliant Scimitar in for a top-of-the-range Elite XS shop mobility scooter and has continued to apply for executive roles in various British and American blue-chip companies, though he has yet to be invited for interview.

Thanks to the generosity of people across Norfolk, £1,358.31 was collected through the King's Trust. The net total raised, after 'overheads', was £156.21, which is currently held at HSBC, earning interest and awaiting distribution to local good causes.

Musmy and HP still live at the bungalow. They now have a new golden retriever puppy called Biscuit, who is the great-niece of Honey. The Commander still visits, every other Sunday, for roast lunch and plenty of pink gin.

The royal carriage, *Zara Reinger*, is currently stabled on Platform 2 at Sheringham Old Station. The carriage contents were sold off to repay monies owed by His Majesty to the Poppy Line Trust, and it is currently being used as a Victorian-themed photo studio.

Pete Fowls married his girlfriend Kate last summer and recently traded his BMW 3 Series in for the latest model. Only he is allowed to open and close the doors, using a chamois leather. He is currently wearing a Letter J rugby shirt, and blames married life for his current lack of drinking performance.

Roy Boy recently bought a new cafe trailer. The Copeman Empire 'By Appointment' crest still takes pride of place next to the serving hatch.

David Chapstone served nine months in a Young Offenders' Institution for assaulting King Nicholas. Upon his release, he got in touch with Nick and arranged to meet up with him at the Crown Inn, to apologise, and buy him a pink gin.

Nick Copeman joined the Royal Navy, but left after two weeks, when he was offered a regional distribution deal for his King Nicholas's Butter Chips. He is currently fine-tuning the recipe, prior to the official launch of the range later this year. HP is the company chairman and Clare is a non-executive director. The manufacturers' marketing team is encouraging Nick to resurrect his royal identity for the pack shot and general promotional purposes. HP has advised against it. Nick is considering the matter carefully.

After a few awkward weeks when they didn't speak to each other much, Nick and Baby Face have made up and are once again best friends. They still get together at Baby Face's caravan every Saturday night for the Chinese Lottery and Nick has offered Baby Face a job at King Nicholas Butter Chips Ltd as a senior promotions director. Baby Face has accepted in principle, and is now negotiating terms. The Gingersnap Clause of 1999 has yet to be invoked.

Nick is still in debt by several thousand pounds, but has got his repayments under control. He is currently living back at the bungalow with Mumsy and HP, to keep his overheads down. He recently bought his third suit, from the Marks & Spencer Sartorial Range, after the royal tailor, Mr Green, died at the age of eighty-two.

Nick still writes to Zara Phillips regularly.

She has yet to reply.

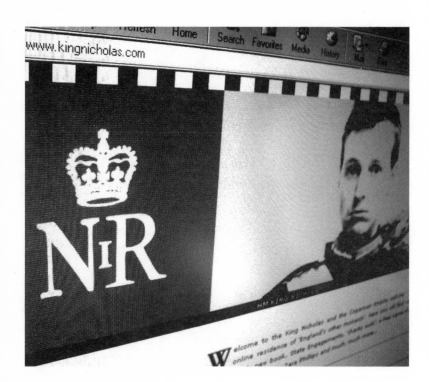

www.kingnicholas.com

Search Favorites Media History

Home

HM KING NICH

Welcome to the King Nicholas and the Clarence House onlin
online residence of England's new monarch. Here you will fin
new book, State Engagements, diaries and a fun comp
new book, Zara Phillips and much, much more

Keep up to date with King Nicholas
and the Copeman Empire at:

www.kingnicholas.com